POEMS.

BY

HENRY TIMROD.

BOSTON:
TICKNOR AND FIELDS.
MDCCCLX.

RIVERSIDE, CAMBRIDGE:
PRINTED BY H. O. HOUGHTON AND COMPANY.

CONTENTS.

SONNETS.

DEDICATION.

TO FAIRY.

Do you recall — I know you do —
A little gift once made to you, —
A simple basket filled with flowers,
All favorites of our Southern bowers?

One was a snowy myrtle-bud,
Another blushed as if with blood,
A third was pink of softest tinge,
Then came a disk with purple fringe.

You took them with a happy smile,
And nursed them for a little while,
And once or twice perhaps you thought
Of the fond messages they brought.

And yet you could not then divine
The promise in that gift of mine,—
In those bright blooms and odors sweet,
I laid this volume at your feet.

At yours, my child, who scarcely know
How much to your dear self I owe—
Too young and innocent as yet
To guess in what consists the debt.

Therefore to you henceforth belong
These Southern asphodels of song,—
Less *my* creations than your own,
What praise they win is yours alone.

For here no fancy finds a place
But is an effluence of your grace;—
And when my songs are sweetest, then
A Dream like you hath touched the pen.

POEMS.

A VISION OF POESY.

PART I.

I.

In a far land and very distant age,
  Ere sprites and fays had bade farewell to earth,
A boy was born of humble parentage;
  The stars that shone upon his lonely birth,
Did seem to promise sovereignty and fame,—
Yet no tradition hath preserved his name.

II.

'Tis said that on the night when he was born,
  A beauteous shape swept slowly through the room;
Its eyes broke on the infant like a morn,
  And his cheek brightened like a rose in bloom;
But as it passed away there followed after
A sigh of pain, and sounds of elvish laughter.

III.

And so his parents deemed him to be blest
  Beyond the lot of mortals; they were poor
As the most timid bird that stored its nest
  With the stray gleanings at their cottage-door:
Yet they contrived to rear their little dove,
And he repaid them with the tenderest love.

IV.

The boy was very beautiful in sooth,
  And as he waxed in years grew lovelier still;
On his fair brow the aureole of truth
  Beamed, — and the purest maidens, with a thrill,
Looked in his eyes, and from their heaven of blue
Saw thoughts like sinless Angels peering through.

V.

The parents gazed upon their boy with pride,
  And all his little ways most closely scanned,
Yet there was something in those ways descried,
  Which neither one could wholly understand, —
A self-withdrawn and independent bliss,
Beside the father's love, the mother's kiss.

VI.

For oft, when he believed himself alone,
  They caught brief snatches of mysterious rhymes,

Which the boy murmured in an undertone,
  Like a pleased bee's in summer; and at times
A strange far look would come into his eyes,
As if he saw a vision in the skies.

VII.

And he upon a simple leaf would pore
  As if its very texture unto him
Had some deep meaning; sometimes by the door,
  From noon until a summer-day grew dim,
He lay and watched the clouds; and to his thought
Night with her stars but fitful slumbers brought.

VIII.

In the long hours of twilight, when the breeze
  Talked in low tones along the woodland rills,
Or the loud North its stormy minstrelsies
  Blent with wild noises from the distant hills,
The boy, — his rosy hand against his ear
Curved like a sea-shell, — hushed as some rapt seer,

IX.

Followed the sounds, and ever and again,
  As the wind came, and went, in storm or play,
He seemed to hearken as to some far strain
  Of mingled voices calling him away;

And they who watched him, held their breath to
trace
The still and fixed attention in his face.

X.

Once, on a cold and loud-voiced winter night,
The three were seated by their cottage-fire, —
The mother watching by its flickering light
The wakeful urchin, and the dozing sire; —
There was a brief, quick motion like a bird's,
And the boy's thought thus rippled into words: —

XI.

"O mother! thou hast taught me many things,
But none I think more beautiful than speech, —
A nobler power than even those broad wings
I used to pray for, when I longed to reach
That distant peak which on our vale looks down,
And wears the star of evening for a crown.

XII.

"But, mother, while our human words are rife
To us with meaning, other sounds there be
Which seem, and are the language of a life,
Around, yet unlike ours; — winds talk; the sea
Murmurs articulately, and the sky
Listens, and answers, though inaudibly.

XIII.

"By stream and spring, in glades and woodlands lone,
Beside our very cot, I've gathered flowers
Inscribed with signs and characters unknown;
But the frail scrolls still baffle all my powers:
What is this language, and where is the key
That opes its weird and wondrous mystery?

XIV.

"The forests know it, and the mountains know,
And it is written in the sunset's dyes;
A revelation to the world below
Is daily going on before our eyes;
And but for sinful thoughts I do not doubt
That we could spell the thrilling secret out.

XV.

"O mother! somewhere on this lovely earth
I lived, and understood that mystic tongue,
But for some reason, to my second birth
Only the dullest memories have clung,
Like that fair tree that ev'n while blossoming,
Keeps the dead berries of a former spring.

XVI.

"Who shall put life in these? — my nightly dreams
Some teacher of supernal powers foretell;

A fair and stately shape appears, which seems
  Bright with all truth ; — and once in a dark dell
Within the forest, unto me there came
A voice that must be her's, which called my name."

XVII.

Puzzled and frightened, wondering more and more,
  The mother heard, but did not comprehend ; —
" So early dallying with forbidden lore !
  Oh, what will chance, and wherein will it end ?
My child ! my child ! " she caught him to her breast,
" Oh, let me kiss these wildering thoughts to rest !

XVIII.

" They cannot come from God, who freely gives
  All that we need to have, or ought to know ;
Beware, my son ! some evil influence strives
  To grieve thy parents, and to work thee woe ; —
Alas ! the vision I misunderstood ! —
It could not be an angel fair and good."

XIX.

And then, in low and tremulous tones, she told
  The story of his birth-night ; — the boy's eyes,
As the wild tale went on, were bright and bold,
  With a weird look that did not seem surprise :
" Perhaps," he said, " this lady and her elves
Will one day come, and take me to themselves."

XX.

"And would'st thou leave us?"—"Dearest mother,
no!
Hush! I will check these thoughts that give thee
pain;
Or, if they flow, as they perchance *must* flow,
At least I will not utter them again;
Hark! the loud Night is calling to the Day!
We should be dreaming!—Mother, let us pray."

XXI.

Thenceforth, whatever impulse stirred below,
In the deep heart beneath that childish breast,
Those lips were sealed, and though the eye would
glow,
Yet the brow wore an air of perfect rest;—
Cheerful, content, with calm though strong control
He shut the temple-portals of his soul.

XXII.

And when too restlessly the mighty throng
Of fancies woke within his teeming mind,
All silently they formed in glorious song,
And floated off unheard, and undivined,
Perchance, not lost,—with many a voiceless prayer
They reached the sky, and found some record
there.

XXIII.

Softly and swiftly sped the quiet days; —
The thoughtful boy has blossomed into youth,
And still no maiden would have feared his gaze,
And still his brow was noble with the truth:
Yet though he masks the pain with pious art,
There burns a restless fever in his heart.

XXIV.

A childish dream is now a deathless need
Which drives him to far hills and distant wilds, —
The solemn faith and fervor of his creed,
Bold as a martyr's, simple as a child's, —
The eagle knew him as she knew the blast,
And the deer did not flee him as he passed.

XXV.

But gentle even in his wildest mood,
Always, and most he loved the bluest weather, —
And in some soft and sunny solitude
Couched like a milder sunshine on the heather,
He communed with the winds, and with the birds,
As if they might have answered him in words.

XXVI.

Deep buried in the forest was a nook,
Remote and quiet as its quiet skies, —

He knew it, sought it, loved it as a book
  Full of his own sweet thoughts and memories;
Dark oaks and fluted chestnuts gathering round,
Pillared and greenly domed a sloping mound,

XXVII.

Whereof — white, purple, azure, golden, red,
  Confused like hues of sunset — the wild flowers
Wove a rich däis; — through crosslights overhead
  Glanced the clear sunshine, fell the fruitful
      showers,
And here the shyest bird would fold her wings, —
Here fled the fairest and the gentlest things.

XXVIII.

Thither, one night of mist and moonlight, came
  The youth, with nothing deeper in his thought
Than to behold beneath the silver flame
  New aspects of his fair and favorite spot; —
A single ray attained the ground, and shed
Just light enough to guide the wanderer's tread.

XXIX.

And high and hushed, arose the stately trees,
  Yet shut within themselves, like dungeons, where
Lay fettered all the secrets of the breeze; —
  Silent, but not as slumbering, all things there

Wore to the youth's aroused imagination
An air of deep and solemn expectation.

XXX.

"Hath Heaven," the youth exclaimed, "a sweeter spot,
Or Earth another like it? — yet ev'n here
The old mystery dwells! — and though I read it not,
Here most I hope it is, or seems so near; —
So many hints come to me, but, alas!
I cannot grasp the shadows as they pass.

XXXI.

"Here, from the very turf beneath me, I
Catch, but just catch, I know not what faint sound,
And darkly guess that from yon silent sky
Float starry emanations to the ground; —
These ears are deaf, these human eyes are blind,
I want a purer heart, a subtler mind.

XXXII.

"Sometimes — could it be fancy? — I have felt
The presence of a spirit who might speak —
As down in lowly reverence I knelt
Its very breath has kissed my burning cheek,

But I in vain have hushed my own to hear
A wing or whisper stir the silent air!"

XXXIII.

Is not the breeze articulate? Hark! Oh, hark!
  A distant murmur, like a voice of floods,
And onward sweeping slowly through the dark,
  Bursts like a call the night-wind from the woods!
Low bow the flowers, the trees fling loose their dreams,
And through the waving roof a fresher moonlight streams.

XXXIV.

"Mortal!" — the word crept slowly round the place
  As if that wind had breathed it! — From no star
Streams that soft lustre on the Dreamer's face, —
  Again a hushing calm! — while faint and far
The breeze goes calling onward through the night, —
Dear God! what vision chains that wide-strained sight?

XXXV.

Over the breathless flowers, and up the slope
  Glides a white cloud of mist, self-moved and slow,
That, pausing at the hillock's moonlit cope,
  Swayed like a flame of silver; — from below

The awe-struck youth with trembling heart beholds
The slow unrolling of its argent folds.

XXXVI.

Yet, his young pulse beats high, and hope grows warm,
As flashing through that cloud of shadowy crape,
With sweep of robes, and then a gleaming arm, —
Slowly developing, at last took shape
A face and form unutterably bright,
That cast another moonshine on the night.

XXXVII.

But for the glory round it, it would seem
Almost a mortal maiden; and the boy,
Unto whom love was yet an innocent dream,
Shivered and crimsoned with an unknown joy; —
As to the young Spring bounds the passionate South,
He could have clasped and kissed her mouth to mouth.

XXXVIII.

Yet, something checked that was and was not dread,
Till in a slow sweet voice the maiden spake;
She was the Fairy of his dreams, she said,
And loved him simply for his human sake;

And that in Heaven, wherefrom she took her
birth,
They called her Poësy, the Angel of the earth.

XXXIX.

" And ever since that immemorial hour,
When the glad morning-stars together sung,
My task hath been beneath a mightier Power,
To keep the world forever fresh and young;
I give it not its fruitage and its green,
But clothe it with a glory all unseen.

XL.

" I sow the germ which buds in human art,
And, with my sister Science, I explore
With light the dark recesses of the heart,
And nerve the will, and teach the wish to soar;
I touch with grace the body's meanest clay,
While noble souls are nobler for my sway.

XLI.

" Before my power the kings of earth have bowed;
I am the voice of Freedom, and the sword
Leaps from its scabbard when I call aloud;
Wherever life in sacrifice is poured,
Wherever martyrs die, or patriots bleed,
I weave the chaplet, and award the meed.

XLII.

"Where Passion stoops, or strays, is cold, or
dead,
I lift from error, or to action thrill;
Or if it rage too madly in its bed,
The tempest hushes at my 'peace! be still!'
I know how far its tides should sink or swell,
And they obey my sceptre, and my spell.

XLIII.

"All lovely things, and gentle,—the sweet laugh
Of children, Girlhood's kiss, and Friendship's
clasp,
The boy that sporteth with the old man's staff,
The baby, and the breast its fingers grasp,—
All that exalts the grounds of happiness,
All griefs that hallow, and all joys that bless,

XLIV.

"To me are sacred; at my holy shrine
Love breathes its latest dreams, its earliest
hints;
I turn life's tasteless waters into wine,
And flush them through and through with purple
tints;—
Wherever Earth is fair, and Heaven looks down,
I rear my altars, and I wear my crown.

XLV.

"I am the unseen spirit thou hast sought,
I woke those shadowy questionings that vex
Thy young mind, lost in its own cloud of thought,
And rouse the soul they trouble and perplex;
I filled thy days with visions, and thy nights
Blessed with all sweetest sounds, and fairy sights.

XLVI.

"Not here, not in this world, may I disclose
The mysteries in which this life is hearsed,
Some doubts there be that with some earthly woes,
By Death alone shall wholly be dispersed;
Yet on those very doubts from this low sod
Thy soul shall pass beyond the stars to God.

XLVII.

"And so to knowledge, climbing grade by grade,
Thou shalt attain whatever mortals can,
And what thou may'st discover, by my aid
Thou shalt translate unto thy brother, man;
And men shall bless the power that flings a ray
Into their night from thy diviner day.

XLVIII.

"For from thy lofty height, thy words shall fall
Upon their spirits, like bright cataracts

That front a sunrise; thou shalt hear them call
  Amid their endless wastes of arid facts,
As wearily they plod their way along,
Upon the rhythmic zephyrs of thy song.

XLIX.

"All this is in thy reach, but much depends
  Upon thyself; — thy future I await;
I give the genius, point the proper ends,
  But the true bard is his own only Fate:
Into thy soul my soul have I infused,
But even my loftiest powers may be abused.

L.

"The Poet owes a high, and holy debt,
  Which, if he feel, he craves not to be heard
For the poor boon of praise, or place, nor yet
  Does the mere joy of song, as with the bird
Of many voices, prompt the choral lay
That cheers that gentle pilgrim on his way.

LI.

"Nor may he always sweep the passionate lyre,
  Which is his heart, only for such relief
As an impatient spirit may desire; —
  Lest from the grave which hides a private grief
The spells of song call up some pallid wraith
To blast, or ban a mortal hope or faith.

LII.

"Yet over his deep soul with all its crowd
  Of varying hopes and fears, still must he brood, —
As from its azure height a tranquil cloud
  Watches its own bright changes in the flood; —
Self-reading, not self-loving, — they are twain, —
And sounding, while he mourns, the depths of pain.

LIII.

"Thus shall his songs attain the common breast,
  Dyed in his own life's blood, the sign and seal,
Even as the thorns which are the martyr's crest,
  Which shall attest his office, and appeal
Unto the universal human heart
In sanction of his mission and his art.

LIV.

"Much yet remains unsaid; — pure he must be;
  Oh, blessèd are the pure! for they shall hear
Where others hear not, see, where others see
  With a dazed vision: who have drawn most near
My shrine, have ever brought a spirit cased
And mailèd in a body clean and chaste.

LV.

"The Poet to the whole wide world belongs
  Even as the teacher is the child's; — I said

No selfish aim should ever mar his songs,
  But self wears many guises; men may wed
Self in another, and the soul may be
Self to its centre, all unconsciously.

LVI.

"And therefore must the Poet watch, lest he,
  In the long struggle of his life, should take
Stains which he might not notice; he must flee
  Falsehood, however winsome, and forsake
All for the Truth, assured that Truth alone
Is Beauty, and can make him all my own.

LVII.

"And he must be as armèd warrior strong,
  And he must be as gentle as a girl,
And he must front, and sometimes suffer wrong,
  With brow unbent, and lip untaught to curl,
For wrath, and scorn, and pride, however just,
Filleth the soul's clear eyes with earthly dust."

PART II.

THE story came to me, — it recks not whence, —
In fragments; Oh! if I could tell it all,
If human speech indeed could tell it all,
'Twere not a whit less wondrous, than if I
Should find, untouched in leaf and stem, and bright
As when it bloomed three thousand years ago
On some Idalian slope, a perfect rose.
Alas! a leaf or two, and they perchance
Scarce worth the hiving, one or two dead leaves
Are the sole harvest of a summer's toil.
There was a moment, ne'er to be recalled,
When to the Poet's hope within my heart,
They wore a tint like life's, but in my hand,
I know not why, they withered. I have heard
Somewhere, of some dead Monarch, from the tomb
Where he had slept a century and more,
Brought forth, that when the coffin was laid bare,
Albeit the body in its mouldering robes
Was fleshless, yet one feature still remained
Perfect, or perfect seemed at least; the eyes
Gleamed for a second on the startled crowd,
And then went out in ashes. Even thus
The story, when I drew it from the grave

Where it had lain so long, did seem, I thought,
Not wholly lifeless, but even while I gazed
To fix its features on my heart, and called
The world to wonder with me, lo! it proved
I looked upon a corpse!

What further passed
In that lone forest nook, how much was taught,
How much was only hinted, and how much
Was left in utter darkness, what the youth
Promised, if promise were required, to do
Or strive for, what the gifts he bore away, —
Or added powers or blessings, — how at last,
The vision ended and he sought his home,
How lived there, and how long, and when he passed
Into the busy world to seek his fate,
I know not, and if any ever knew,
The tale hath perished from the earth, for here
The slender thread on which my song is strung
Breaks off, and many after years of life
Are lost to sight, the life to reappear
Only towards its close, — as of a dream
We catch the end, and opening, but forget
That which had joined them in the dreaming brain;
Or as a mountain with a belt of mist
That shows his base, and far above, a peak
With a blue plume of pines.

Some scattered links
I may have found, mere hints in sooth, of what
He did and suffered under heaven; but I
Choose not of doubtful shades and bits of light
To weave a specious tale. Enough to say,
If I have read aright, that on this earth
He was a wanderer; — once, and yet again
He crossed it, coming from the distant morn
Toward the sunset; and in every land,
And unto every people did he sing
Of all he thought, and all he dreamed and hoped;
But, or because the people were intent
On other themes, or they were not prepared
To dream his dreams, or think the thoughts he thought,
Or that, not being as other men, he touched
No chord that vibrated from heart to heart,
The people would not hear, or, hearing, turned
And went their way unheedful. Something, too,
Of love successless, and not wisely placed,
I gleaned; and from the wreck of those sad years
Three brief, but pregnant scenes remain: in one,
He stands, a crowd about him, in a street
Of some great populous town, and to the crowd
He speaks, but seems to see it not; his eyes
Seek only the far distance, where the street
A golden sunset closes, or they turn

Inward, as searching thought, nor does he mark
The sneers of some, the listlessness of most,
Nor ev'n the few who seem to weigh his speech.
And next a softer scene — the time is morn —
Rises, — a cottage in a wood, and near,
A troop of maidens dancing fairily,
Who, on a sudden, and as if they spied
Some monstrous creature unakin to men,
Break and dispart, and as they fly, they shriek
"Away! the wizard! see, he comes, he comes!"
And the next moment, with the reverent step
Of courtesy too gentle to reproach,
Even the groundless fears which do him wrong,
The weary Wanderer passes sadly by.
And yet, once more the picture changes; — he
Paces a bare black beach alone; in front
A wintry sea, o'er which a storm of rain,
Like the dark shadow of some world-wide wing,
Goes sweeping, — yet he heeds it not, but looks
A spirit with the spirits of the winds,
Wild revellers, but his sole companions now,
Communing, as a friend communes with friends.

PART III.

I.

It is not winter yet, but that sweet time
In autumn when the first cool days are passed;
A week ago, the leaves were hoar with rime,
And some have dropped before the North-Wind's blast;
But the mild hours are back, and at mid-noon,
The day hath all the genial warmth of June.

II.

Betwixt the forest stems, a thick blue air
Shuts the long vistas of those deep arcades;
Here, there are glints of purple sky, and there,
A dim pink sunshine lights the breezeless glades;
These, we must leave for one familiar nook;—
Come, but let no cold worldling enter!—look!

III.

What slender form lies stretched along the mound?
Can it be *his*, the Wanderer's, with that brow
Gray in its prime, those eyes that wander round
Listlessly, with a jaded glance that now
Seems to see nothing where it rests, and then
Pores on each trivial object in its ken?

IV.

See how a gentle maid's wan fingers clasp
  The last fond love-notes of some faithless hand;
Thus with a transient interest, his weak grasp
  Gathers the leaves around, which dropped, half scanned,
He gathers yet once more; — heart-touching freaks! —
Is the old dream upon him? hush! he speaks!

V.

"Once more, once more, after long pain and toil,
  And yet not long, if I should count by years,
I breathe my native air, and tread the soil
  I trod in childhood; if I shed no tears,
No happy tears, 'tis that their fount is dry,
And joy that cannot weep must sigh, must sigh.

VI.

"These leaves, my boyish books in days of yore,
  When, as the weeks sped by, I seemed to stand
Ever upon the brink of some wild lore, —
  These leaves shall make my bed, and — for the hand
Of God is on me, chilling brain and breath, —
I shall not ask a softer couch in death.

VII.

"Here was it that I saw, or dreamed I saw —
I know not which — that shape of love and light;
Spirit of Song! have I not owned thy law? —
Have I not taught, or striven to teach the right,
And kept my heart as clean, my life as sweet,
As mortals may, when mortals mortals meet?

VIII.

"Thou know'st how I went forth, my youthful breast
On fire with thee, amid the paths of men; —
Once in my wanderings, my lone footsteps pressed
A mountain forest; — in a sombre glen,
Down which its thunderous boom a cataract flung,
A little bird, unheeded, built and sung.

IX.

"So fell my voice amid the whirl and rush
Of human passions; if unto my art
Sorrow hath sometimes owed a gentler gush,
I know it not; if any Poet-heart
Hath kindled at my songs its light divine,
I know it not; no ray came back to mine!

X.

"Alone in crowds, once more I sought to make
Of senseless things my friends; the clouds that
burn

Above the sunset, and the flowers that shake
  Their odors in the wind, — these would not turn
Their faces from me; far from cities, I
Forgot the scornful world that passed me by.

XI.

"Yet even the world's cold slights I might have borne,
  Nor fled, though sorrowing; but I shrunk at last
When one sweet face, too sweet, I thought, for scorn,
  Looked scornfully upon me; then I passed
From all that youth had dreamed or manhood planned,
Into the self that none would understand.

XII.

"She was — I never wronged her womanhood
  By crowning it with praises not her own —
She was all earth's, and earth's too in that mood,
  When she brings forth her fairest; I atone
Now, in this fading brow and failing frame,
That such a soul such soul as mine could tame.

XIII.

"Clay to its kindred clay! — I loved in sooth
  Too deeply and too purely to be blest;
With something more of lust and less of truth,

She would have sunk all blushes on my breast,
And — but I must not blame her — in my ear
Death whispers! and the end, thank God! draws near!"

XIV.

Hist! on the perfect silence of the place
Comes, and dies off a sound like far-off rain
With voices mingled; on the Poet's face
A shadow, where no shadow should have lain,
Falls the next moment: nothing meets his sight,
Yet, something moves betwixt him and the light.

XV.

And a voice murmurs, "Wonder not, but hear!
Me, to behold again, thou need'st not seek;
Yet by the dim-felt influence on the air,
And by the mystic shadow on thy cheek,
Know, though thou may'st not touch with fleshly hands,
The genius of thy life beside thee stands!

XVI.

"Unto no fault, O weary-hearted one!
Unto no fault of man's thou ow'st thy fate;
All human hearts that beat this earth upon,
All human thoughts and human passions wait

Upon the genuine bard, to him belong,
And help in their own way the Poet's song.

XVII.

"How blame the world? for the world hast thou
wrought?
Or, wast thou but as one who aims to fling
The weight of some unutterable thought
Down like a burden? — what from questioning
Too subtly thy own spirit, and to speech
But half subduing themes beyond the reach

XVIII.

"Of mortal reason, what from living much
In that dark world of shadows, where the soul
Wanders bewildered, striving still to clutch,
Yet never clutching once, a shadowy goal,
Which always flies, and while it flies, seems near, —
Thy songs were riddles hard to mortal ear.

XIX.

"This was the hidden selfishness that marred
Thy teachings ever; this the false key-note
That on such souls as might have loved thee jarred
Like an unearthly language; thou did'st float
On a strange water; those who stood on land
Gazed, but they could not leave their beaten strand.

XX.

"Your elements were different, and apart,
—The world's and thine;—and even in those intense
And watchful broodings o'er thy inmost heart,
It was thy own peculiar difference
That thou did'st seek,—nor did'st thou care to find
Aught that would bring thee nearer to thy kind.

XXI.

"Not thus the Poet who in blood and brain
Would represent his race and speak for all,
Weaves the bright woof of that impassioned strain
Which drapes, as if for some high festival
Of pure delights,—whence few of human birth
May rightly be shut out,—the common earth.

XXII.

"As the same law that moulds a planet rounds
A drop of dew, so the great Poet spheres
Worlds in himself; no selfish limit bounds
A sympathy that folds all characters,
All ranks, all passions, and all life almost
In its wide circle. Like some noble host,

XXIII.

"He spreads the riches of his soul, and bids
Partake who will;—Age has its saws of truth,

And love is for the maiden's drooping lids,
  And words of passion for the earnest youth;
Wisdom for all; and when it seeks relief,
Tears, and their solace for the heart of grief.

XXIV.

"Nor less on him than thee, the mysteries
  Within him, and about him ever weigh,—
The meanings in the stars, and in the breeze,
  The fairy wonders of the common day,
Truths that the merest point removes from reach,
And thoughts that pause upon the brink of speech;

XXV.

"But on the surface of his song, *these* lie
  As shadows, not as darkness; and alway
Even though it breathe the secrets of the sky,
  There is a human purpose in the lay;
As some tall fir that whispers to the stars
Shields at its base a cotter's lattice-bars.

XXVI.

"Even such my Poet!—for thou still art mine!—
  Thou might'st have been, and now have calmly died,
A Priest, and not a victim at the shrine;
  Alas! yet was it all thy fault? I chide,

Perchance, *myself* within thee, and the fate
To which thy power was solely consecrate.

XXVII.

"Thy life hath not been wholly without use,
  Albeit that use is partly hidden now;
In thy unmingled scorn of any truce
  With this world's specious falsehoods, often thou
Hast uttered, through some all unworldly song,
Truths that for man might else have slumbered long.

XXVIII.

"And these not always vainly on the crowd
  Have fallen; some are cherished now, and some
In mystic phrases wrapped as in a shroud,
  Wait the diviner, who as yet is dumb
Upon the breast of God — the gate of birth
Closed on a dreamless ignorance of earth.

XXIX.

"And therefore, though thy name shall pass away,
  Even as a cloud that hath wept all its showers,
Yet as that cloud shall live again one day
  In the glad grass, and in the happy flowers,
So in thy thoughts, though clothed in sweeter rhymes,
Thy life shall bear its flowers in future times."

THE PAST.

TO-DAY'S most trivial act may hold the seed
 Of future fruitfulness, or future dearth;—
Oh, cherish always every word and deed!
 The simplest record of thyself hath worth.

If thou hast ever slighted one old thought,
 Beware lest Grief enforce the truth at last;
The time must come wherein thou shalt be taught,
 The value and the beauty of the Past.

Not merely as a warner and a guide,
 "A voice behind thee," sounding to the strife;
But something never to be put aside,
 A part and parcel of thy present life.

Not as a distant and a darkened sky,
 Through which the stars peep, and the moonbeams
 glow;
But a surrounding atmosphere, whereby
 We live and breathe, sustained in pain and woe.

A Fairy-land, where joy and sorrow kiss —
  Each still to each corrective and relief —
Where dim delights are brightened into bliss,
  And nothing wholly perishes but Grief.

Ah, me! — not dies — no more than spirit dies;
  But in a change like death is clothed with wings, —
A serious angel, with entrancèd eyes,
  Looking to far-off and celestial things.

PRÆCEPTOR AMAT.

It is time (it *was* time long ago) I should sever
This chain — why I wear it I know not — forever!
Yet I cling to the bond, ev'n while sick of the
mask
I must wear, as of one whom his commonplace
task
And proof-armor of dullness have steeled to her
charms!
Ah! how lovely she looked as she flung from her
arms,
In heaps to this table, (now starred with the stains
Of her booty yet wet with those yesterday rains,)
These roses and lilies, and — what? let me see!
Then was off in a moment, but turned with a
glee,
That lit her sweet face as with moonlight, to say,
As 'twas almost too late for a lesson to-day,
She meant to usurp, for this morning at least,
My office of Tutor; and 'stead of a feast
Of such mouthfuls as *poluphloisboio thalasses*,
With which I fed *her*, I should study the grasses,

(Love-grasses she called them,) the buds, and the
flowers,
Of which I know nothing; and if "with *my* powers,"
I did not learn all she could teach in that time,
And thank her, perhaps, in a sweet English rhyme,
If I did not do this, — and she flung back her hair,
And shook her bright head with a menacing air —
She'd be — oh! she'd be — a real Saracen Omar
To a certain much-valued edition of Homer!
But these flowers! I believe I could number as
soon
The shadowy thoughts of a last summer's noon,
Or recall with their phases, each one after one,
The clouds that came down to the death of the
Sun,
Cirrus, Stratus, or Nimbus, some evening last year,
As unravel the web of one genus! Why, there,
As they lie by my desk in that glistering heap,
All tangled together like dreams in the sleep
Of a bliss-fevered heart, I might turn them and turn
Till night, in a puzzle of pleasure, and learn
Not a fact, not a secret I prize half so much,
As, how rough is this leaf when I think of her
touch!
There's one now, blown yonder! what *can* be its
name?
A topaz wine-colored! the wine in a flame!

And another that's hued like the pulp of a melon,
But sprinkled all o'er as with seed-pearls of Ceylon!
And a third! its white petals just clouded with pink!
And a fourth, that blue star! and then *this* too; — I think
If one brought me this moment an amethyst cup,
From which, through a liquor of amber, looked up,
With a glow as of eyes in their elfin-like lustre,
Stones culled from all lands in a sunshiny cluster,
From the ruby that burns in the sands of Mysore
To the beryl of Daunia, with gems from the core
Of the mountains of Persia (I talk like a boy
In the flush of some new, and yet half-tasted joy;)
But I think if that cup and its jewels together
Were placed by the side of this child of the weather,
(*This* one which she touched with her mouth, and let slip
From her fingers by chance, as her exquisite lip,
With a music befitting the language divine,
Gave the roll of the Greek's multitudinous line)
I should take — *not* the gems — but enough — let me shut
In the blossom that woke it, my folly, and put
Both away in my bosom, — there, in a heart-niche,
One shall outlive the other, — is't hard to tell which?
In the name of all starry and beautiful things,
What is it? the cross in the centre, these rings,

And the petals that shoot in an intricate maze,
From the disk which is lilac (or purple?) like rays
In a blue Aureole!

And so now will she wot,
When I sit by her side with my brows in a knot,
And praise her so calmly, or chide her perhaps,
If her words falter once in their musical lapse,
As I've done, I confess, just to gaze at a flush
In the white of her throat, or to watch the quick
rush
Of the tear she sheds smiling, as, drooping her
curls
O'er that book I keep shrined like a casket of
pearls,
She reads on in a voice of such tremulous sweet-
ness,
That (in spite of some faults) I am forced, in
discreetness,
To silence, lest mine growing hoarse, should betray
What I must not reveal, — will she guess now, I
say,
How, for all his grave looks, the stern, passionless
Tutor,
With more than the love of her youthfullest suitor,
Is hiding somewhere in the shroud of his vest,
By a heart that is beating wild wings in its nest,

This flower, thrown aside in the sport of a minute,
And which *he* holds as dear as though folded within it,
Lay the germ of the bliss that he dreams of! Ah, me!
It is hard to love thus, yet to seem and to be
A thing for indifference, faint praise, or cold blame,
When you long (by the right of deep passion, the claim
On the loved of the loving, at least to be heard)
To take the white hand, and with glance, touch, and word,
Burn your way to the heart! That her step on the stair!
Be still thou fond flutterer!

How little I care
For your favorites, see! they are all of them, look!
On the spot where they fell, and —— but here is your book!

DREAMS.

WHO first said "false as dreams"? Not one who saw
Into the wild and wondrous world they sway;
No thinker who hath read their mystic law;
No Poet who hath weaved them in his lay.

Else had he known that through the human breast
Cross and recross a thousand fleeting gleams,
That, passed unnoticed in the day's unrest,
Come out at night, like stars, in shining dreams;

That minds too busy or too dull to mark
The dim suggestions of the noisier hours,
By dreams in the deep silence of the dark,
Are roused at midnight with their folded powers.

Like that old fount beneath Dodona's oaks,
That, dry and voiceless in the garish noon,
When the calm night arose with modest looks,
Caught with full wave the sparkle of the moon.

If, now and then, a ghastly shape glide in,
Or burst the gate of Sleep with iron keys,
It is the ghost of some forgotten sin
We failed to exorcise on bended knees.

And that sweet face which only yesternight
Came to thy solace, Dreamer, (did'st thou read
The blessing in its eyes of tearful light?)
Was but the spirit of some gentle deed.

Come in what shape they may, our dreams in sooth,
Their gods, their fays, their demons, and their elves,
Are allegories with deep hearts of truth
That tell us solemn secrets of ourselves.

THE PROBLEM.

Not to win thy favor, maiden, not to steal away
thy heart,
Have I ever sought thy presence, ever stooped to
any art;
Thou wast but a 'wildering problem, which I aimed
to solve, and then
Make it matter for my note-book, or a picture for
my pen;—
So, I daily conned thee over, thinking it no dan-
gerous task,
Peeping underneath thy lashes, peering underneath
thy mask,—
For thou wear'st one,—no denial!—there is much
within thine eyes;
But those stars have other secrets than are patent
in their skies.
And I read thee, read thee closely, every grace
and every sin,
Looked behind the outward seeming to the strange
wild world within,

Where thy future self is forming, where I saw —
no matter what! —
There was something less than angel, there was
many an earthly spot.
Yet so beautiful thy errors that I had no heart
for blame,
And thy virtues made thee dearer than my dearest
hopes of fame,
All so blended, that in wishing one peculiar trait
removed,
We indeed might make thee better, but less lovely
and less loved.
All my mind was in the study, — so two thrilling
fortnights passed, —
All my mind was in the study — till my heart
was touched at last.
Well! and then the book was finished; the absorbing
task was done!
I awoke as one who had been dreaming in a
noonday sun;
With a fever on my forehead, and a throbbing in
my brain;
In my soul delirious wishes, in my heart a lasting
pain;
Yet so hopeless, yet so cureless, — as in every great
despair, —
I was very calm and silent, and I never stooped
to prayer,

Like a sick man unattended, reckless of the coming
death,
Only for he knows it certain, and he feels no
sister's breath.
All the while as by an ATÉ, with no pity in her
face,
Yet with eyes of witching beauty, and with form
of matchless grace,
I was haunted by thy presence — oh! for weary
nights and days,
I was haunted by thy spirit, I was troubled by
thy gaze.
And the question which to answer I had taxed a
subtle brain,
What thou art, and what thou wilt be, came again
and yet again,
With its opposite deductions, it recurred a thousand
times,
Like a coward's apprehensions, like a madman's
favorite rhymes.
But to-night my thoughts flow calmer — in thy room
I think I stand,
See a fair white page before thee, and a pen
within thy hand;
And thy fingers sweep the paper, and a light is
in thine eyes,
Whilst I read thy secret fancies, whilst I hear thy
secret sighs.

What they are I will not whisper — those are lovely,
these are deep —
But *one* name is left unwritten — *that* is only
breathed in sleep.
Is it wonder that my passion bursts at once from
out its nest?
I have bent my knee before thee, and my love is
all confessed;
Though I knew that name unwritten was another
name than mine,
Though I felt those sighs half murmured — what I
could but half divine.
Aye! I hear thy haughty answer! Aye! I see
thy proud lip curl!
"What presumption, and what folly!" — why, I only
love a girl
With some very winning graces, with some very
noble traits,
But no better than a thousand who have bent to
humbler fates.
That I ask not; I have, maiden, just as haught a
soul as thine;
If thou think'st thy place above me, thou shalt
never stoop to mine.
Yet as long as blood runs redly, yet as long as
mental worth,
Is a nobler gift than fortune, is a holier thing
than birth,

I will claim the right to utter, to the high and to the low,
That I love them, or I hate them, that I am a friend or foe.
Nor shall any slight unman me, — I have yet some little strength,
Yet my songs shall sound as sweetly, yet a power be mine at length!
Then, oh, then! — but moans are idle — hear me, pitying saints above!
With a chaplet on my forehead, I will justify my love;
And perhaps when thou art leaning on some less devoted breast,
Thou shalt murmur, "He was worthier than my blinded spirit guessed."

Turning to the stars that yonder roll through tranquil depths of space, —
There, oh, God! ev'n there I see thee, and I meet that earnest face!
Siren! hence! I seldom pray, but let me pass this night in prayer, —
God! thou know'st my heart is earthly! God! my stormy heart is bare!
But I need thy consolation, — there is that within my soul

Which should wake thy tender mercy, which requires
thy strong control;
In this world where I must wander without any
hand in mine,
When too bold, or when too feeble, Father! wilt
thou lend me thine!
Touch my songs with holier feeling, touch my lips
with sacred fire,
Give me strength to calm the throbbings of this
passionate desire!
I demand no earthly blessings, I demand no worldly
joys —
I would leave these tainted pleasures unto women
and to boys;
Only in thy strong protection, only shielded by thy
love,
Let me give the world a memory, let me lift my
soul above —
And when shadows close around me, and when
death is on my brow,
O! forgive me if I whisper that dear name I
whisper now.

THE ARCTIC VOYAGER.

Shall I desist, twice baffled? Once by land,
And once by sea, I fought and strove with storms,
All shades of danger, tides and weary calms,
Head-currents, cold and famine, savage beasts,
And men more savage; all the while my face
Looked northward toward the pole; if mortal strength
Could have sustained me, I had never turned
Back till I saw the star which never sets
Freeze in the Arctic zenith. That I failed
To solve the mysteries of the ice-bound world,
Was not because I faltered in the quest.
Witness those pathless forests which conceal
The bones of perished comrades, that long march,
Blood-tracked o'er flint and snow, and one dread night,
By Athabasca, when a cherished life
Flowed, to give life to others. This, and worse,
I suffered, — let it pass — it has not tamed
My spirit nor the faith which was my strength.

Despite of waning years, despite the world
Which doubts, the few who dare, I purpose now —
A purpose long and thoughtfully revolved,
Through all its grounds of reasonable hope —
To seek beyond the ice which guards the Pole,
A sea of open water; for I hold,
Not without proofs, that such a sea exists,
And may be reached, though since this earth was made,
No keel hath ploughed it, and to mortal ear,
No wind hath told its secrets . . . With this tide,
I sail; if all be well, this very moon
Shall see my ship beyond the southern Cape
Of Greenland, and far up the bay through which,
With diamond spire and gorgeous pinnacle,
The fleets of Winter pass to warmer seas.
Whether, my hardy shipmates! we shall reach
Our bourne, and come with tales of wonder back,
Or whether we shall lose the precious time,
Locked in thick ice, or whether some strange fate
Shall end us all, I know not; but I know
A lofty hope, if earnestly pursued,
Is its own crown, and never in this life
Is labor fruitless. What must be, must be;
I shall not count the chances — sure that all
A prudent foresight asks, we shall not want,
And all that bold and patient hearts can do,
Ye will not leave undone. The rest is God's!

A YEAR'S COURTSHIP.

I SAW her, Harry, first, in March ; —
You know the street that leadeth down
By the old bridge's crumbling arch ? —
Just where it leaves the dusty town,

A lonely house stands grim and dark —
You've seen it? — then I need not say
How quaint the place is — did you mark
An ivied window? well, one day,

I, chasing some forgotten dream,
And in a poet's idlest mood,
Caught, as I passed, a white hand's gleam, —
A shutter opened ; — there she stood

Training the ivy to its prop.
Two blue eyes and a brow of snow
Flashed down upon me — did I stop ? —
She says I did — I do not know.

But all that day did something glow
  Just where the heart beats; frail and slight,
A germ had slipped its shell, and now
  Was pushing softly for the light.

And April saw me at her feet,
  Dear month of sunshine and of rain!
My very fears were sometimes sweet,
  And hope was often touched with pain.

For she was frank, and she was coy, —
  A wilful April in her ways;
And in a dream of doubtful joy
  I passed some truly April days.

May came, and on that arch, sweet mouth,
  The smile was graver in its play,
And, softening with the softening South,
  My April melted into May.

She loved me, yet my heart *would* doubt,
  And ere I spoke, the month was June, —
One warm still night we wandered out
  To watch a slowly setting moon.

Something which I saw not — my eyes
  Were not on heaven — a star perchance,

Or some bright drapery of the skies,
  Had caught her earnest, upward glance.

And as she paused — Hal! we have played
  Upon the very spot — a fir
Just touched me with its dreamy shade,
  But the full moonlight fell on her.

And as she paused, — I know not why, —
  I longed to speak, yet could not speak;
The bashful are the boldest, — I ——
  I stooped and gently kissed her cheek.

A murmur (else some fragrant air
  Stirred softly) and the faintest start!
O Hal! we were the happiest pair!
  O Hal! I clasped her heart to heart!

And kissed away some tears that gushed!
  But how she trembled, timid dove!
When my soul broke its silence, flushed
  With a whole burning June of love.

Since then a happy year hath sped
  Through months that seemed all June and May,
And soon a March sun, overhead,
  Will usher in the crowning day.

Twelve blessèd moons that seemed to glow
  All summer, Hal! — my peerless Kate!
She is the dearest — "Angel"? — no!
  Thank God! — but you shall see her, — wait.

So, all is told! I count on thee
  To see the priest, Hal! Pass the wine!
Here's to my darling wife to be!
  And here's to — when thou find'st her — thine!

DRAMATIC FRAGMENT.

Let the boy have his will! I tell thee, brother,
We treat these little ones too much like flowers,
Training them, in blind selfishness, to deck
Sticks of our poor setting, when they might,
If left to clamber where themselves incline,
Find nobler props to cling to, fitter place,
And sweeter air to bloom in. It is wrong, —
Thou striv'st to sow with feelings all thine own,
With thoughts and hopes, anxieties and aims,
Born of thine own peculiar self, and fed
Upon a certain round of circumstance,
A soul as different and distinct from thine,
As love of goodness is from love of glory,
Or noble poesy from noble prose.
I could forgive thee, if thou wast of them
Who do their fated parts in this world's business,
Scarce knowing how or why, — for common minds
See not the difference 'twixt themselves and others, —
But thou, *thou* with the visions which thy youth
did cherish,

Substantialized upon thy regal brow,
Should'st boast a deeper insight. We are born,
It is my faith, in miniature completeness,
And like each other only in our weakness.
Even with our mother's milk upon our lips,
Our smiles have different meanings, and our hands
Press with *degrees* of softness to her bosom.
It is not change, — whatever in the heart
That wears its semblance, we, in looking back,
With gratulation or regret, perceive, —
It is not change we undergo, but only
Growth or development. Yes! what is childhood,
But after all a sort of golden daylight,
A beautiful and blessèd wealth of sunshine,
Wherein the powers and passions of the soul,
Sleep starlike but existent, till the night
Of gathering years shall call the slumberers forth,
And they rise up in glory? Early grief,
A shadow like the darkness of eclipse,
Hath sometimes waked them sooner.

MADELINE.

O LADY! if, until this hour,
I've gazed in those bewildering eyes,
Yet never owned their touching power,
But when thou could'st not hear my sighs;
It has not been that love has slept
One single moment in my soul,
Or that on lip or look I kept
A stern and stoical control;
But that I saw, but that I felt,
In every tone and glance of thine,
Whate'er they spoke, where'er they dwelt,
How small, how poor a part was mine;
And that I deeply, dearly knew,
That hidden, hopeless love confessed,
The fatal words would lose me, too,
Even the weak friendship I possessed.

And so, I masked my secret well;
The very love within my breast,
Became the strange, but potent spell

By which I forced it into rest.
Yet there were times, I scarce know how,
These eager lips refrained to speak, —
Some kindly smile would light thy brow,
And I grew passionate and weak;
The secret sparkled at my eyes,
And love but half repressed its sighs, —
Then had I gazed an instant more,
Or dwelt one moment on that brow,
I might have changed the smile it wore,
To what perhaps it weareth now;
And spite of all I feared to meet,
Confessed that passion at thy feet.
To save my heart, to spare thine own,
There was one remedy alone.
I fled, I shunned thy very touch, —
It cost me much, O God! how much!
But, if some burning tears were shed,
Lady! I let them freely flow;
At least, they left unbreathed, unsaid,
A worse and wilder woe.

But now, — *now* that we part indeed,
And that I may not think as then
That as I wish, or as I need,
I may return again, —
Now that for months, perhaps for years —

I see no limit in my fears —
My home shall be some distant spot,
Where thou — where even thy name is not, —
And since I shall not see the frown,
Such wild, mad language must bring down, —
Could I — albeit I may not sue
  In hope to bend thy steadfast will —
Could I have breathed this word, adieu,
  And kept my secret still?

Doubtless thou know'st the Hebrew story —
  The tale 's with me a favorite one —
How Raphael left the Courts of Glory,
  And walked with Judah's honored Son;
And how the twain together dwelt,
  And how they talked upon the road,
How often too they must have knelt
  As equals to the same kind God;
And still the mortal never guessed,
How much and deeply he was blessed,
Till when — the Angel's mission done —
  The spell which drew him earthwards, riven —
The lover saved — the maiden won —
  He plumed again his wings for Heaven;
O Madeline! as unaware
Thou hast been followed everywhere,
  And girt and guarded by a love,

As warm, as tender in its care,
As pure, ay, powerful in prayer,
  As any saint above!
Like the bright inmate of the skies,
It only looked with friendly eyes,
And still had worn the illusive guise,
  And thus at least been half concealed;
But at this parting, painful hour,
It spreads its wings, unfolds its power,
  And stands, like Raphael, revealed.

More, Lady! I would wish to speak,—
But it were vain, and words are weak,
And now that I have bared my breast,
Perchance thou wilt infer the rest.
So, so, farewell! I need not say
  I look, I ask for no reply,
The cold and scarcely pitying "nay"
  I read in that unmelted eye;
Yet one dear favor, let me pray!
  Days, months, however slow to me,
Must drag at last their length away,
  And I return — if not to thee —
At least to breathe the same sweet air
That woos thy lips and waves thy hair.
Oh, then! — these daring lines forgot —
Look, speak as thou hadst read them not.

So, Lady, may I still retain
A right I would not lose again,
For all that gold or guilt can buy,
Or all that Heaven itself deny,
A right such love may justly claim,
Of seeing thee in friendship's name.
Give me but this, and still at whiles,
A portion of thy faintest smiles,
  It were enough to bless;
I may not, dare not ask for more
Than boon so rich, and yet so poor,
  But I should die with less.

THE SUMMER BOWER.

It is a place whither I've often gone
For peace, and found it, secret, hushed and cool,
A beautiful recess in neighboring woods.
Trees of the soberest hues, thick-leaved and tall,
Arch it o'erhead, and girt it with their brown
Trunks, interspersed with plants of humbler growth,
A covert framing, natural and wild,
Domelike and dim; though nowhere so enclosed
But that the gentlest breezes reach the spot
Unwearied and unweakened. Other sounds
Than the low dreamy melodies of winds,
And the soft notes of birds, of that lone nook
Are transient and unfrequent visitors.
Yet if the day be calm, not often then,
Whilst the high pines in one another's arms
Sleep, you may sometimes with unstartled ear
Catch the far fall of voices, how remote
You know not, and you do not care to know.
Verdant and soft the turf, but not a flower
Lights the recess, save one, star-shaped and bright,

That sometimes gleams above or 'mid the grass,
A wild flower which I know by sight, not name.
A narrow opening in the branchéd roof,
A single one, is large enough to show,
With that half glimpse a dreamer loves so much,
The blue air and the blessing of the sky.
Thither, I say, I often bend my steps,
When griefs depress, or joys disturb my heart,
And find the calm I look for, or return
Strong with the quiet rapture in my soul.
But one day,
One of those July days when winds have fled
One knows not whither, I, most sick in mind
With thoughts that shall be nameless, yet, no doubt,
Wrong, or at least unhealthful, since though dark
With gloom, and touched with discontent, they had
No adequate excuse, nor cause, nor end,
I, with these thoughts, and on this summer day,
Entered the accustomed haunt, and found for once
No medicinal virtue.
Not a leaf
Stirred with the whispering welcome which I sought,
But in a close and humid atmosphere,
Every fair plant and implicated bough,
Hung lax and lifeless. Something in the place,
Its utter stillness, the unusual heat,
And some more secret influence, I thought,

Weighed on the sense like sin. Above I saw,
Though not a cloud was visible in heaven,
The pallid sky look through a glazéd mist
Like a blue eye in death.
The change perhaps
Was natural enough; my jaundiced sight,
The weather and the time explain it all:
Yet have I drawn a lesson from the spot,
And shrined it in these verses for my heart.
Thenceforth those tranquil precincts I have sought
Not less, and in all shades of various moods,
But always shun to desecrate the spot
By weak repinings, sickly sentiments,
Or inconclusive sorrows. Nature, though
Pure as she was in Eden when her breath
Kissed the white brow of Eve, doth not refuse,
In her own way and with a just reserve,
To sympathize with human suffering;
But for the pains, the fever, and the fret
Engendered of a vain and idle heart,
She hath no solace; and who seeks her when
These be the troubles over which he moans,
Reads in her unreplying lineaments
Rebukes, that, to the guilty consciousness,
Strike like contempt.

SECOND LOVE.

COULD I reveal the secret joy
  Thy presence always with it brings,
The memories so strangely waked
  Of long forgotten things,

The love, the hope, the fear, the grief,
  Which with that voice come back to me, —
Thou wouldst forgive the impassioned gaze
  So often turned on thee.

It was, indeed, that early love,
  But foretaste of this second one, —
The soft light of the morning star
  Before the morning sun.

The same dark beauty in her eyes,
  The same blonde hair and placid brow,
The same deep-meaning, quiet smile
  Thou bendest on me now,

She might have been, she *was* no more
  Than what a prescient hope could make, —
A dear presentiment of thee
  I loved but for thy sake.

A RHAPSODY OF A SOUTHERN WINTER NIGHT.

Oh! dost thou flatter falsely, Hope, sweet Hope?
The day hath scarcely passed that saw thy birth,
Yet thy white wings are plumed to all their scope,
And hour by hour thine eyes have gathered light,
    And grown so large and bright,
That my whole future life unfolds what seems
    Beneath their gentle beams,
A path that leads athwart some guiltless earth,
To which a star is dropping from the night!

        Not many moons ago,
But when these leafless beds were all aglow
With summer's dearest treasures, I
Was reading in this lonely garden-nook;
A July noon was cloudless in the sky,
And soon I put my shallow studies by;
Then sick at heart, and angered by the book,
Which, in good sooth, was but the long-drawn sigh
Of some one who had quarrelled with his kind,
Vexed at the very proofs which I had sought,

And all annoyed while all alert to find
A plausible likeness of my own dark thought,
I cast me down beneath yon oak's wide boughs,
And, shielding with both hands my throbbing brows,
Watched lazily the shadows of my brain.
The feeble tide of peevishness went down,
And left a flat dull waste of dreary pain
Which seemed to clog the blood in every vein;
The world, of course, put on its darkest frown —
In all its realms I saw no mortal crown
Which did not wound or crush some restless head;
And hope, and will, and motive, all were dead.
So, passive as a stone, I felt too low
To claim a kindred with the humblest flower;
Ev'n that would bare its bosom to a shower,
While I henceforth would take no pains to live,
Nor place myself where I might feel or give
A single impulse whence a wish could grow.
There was a tulip scarce a gossamer's throw
Beyond that platanus. A little child,
Most dear to me, looked through the fence and smiled
A hint that I should pluck it for her sake.
Ah, me! I trust I was not well awake —
The voice was very sweet,
Yet a faint languor kept me in my seat.
I saw a pouted lip, a toss, and heard

Some low expostulating tones, but stirred
Not ev'n a leaf's length, till the pretty fay,
Wondering, and half abashed at the wild feat,
Climbed the low pales, and laughed my gloom
away.

And here again, but led by other Powers,
A morning and a golden afternoon,
These happy stars, and yonder setting moon,
Have seen me fleet, unreckoned and untasked,
A round of precious hours.
Oh! here, where in that summer noon I basked,
And strove, with logic frailer than the flowers,
To justify a life of sensuous rest,
A question dear as home or heaven was asked,
And without language answered. I was blest!
Blest with those nameless boons too sweet to trust
Unto the telltale confidence of song.
Love to his own glad self is sometimes coy,
And ev'n thus much doth seem to do him wrong;
While in the fears which chasten mortal joy,
Is one that shuts the lips, lest speech too free,
With the cold touch of hard reality,
Should turn its priceless jewels into dust.

Since that long kiss which closed the morning's
talk,

I have not strayed beyond this garden walk.
As yet a vague delight is all I know,
A sense of joy so wild 'tis almost pain,
And like a trouble drives me to and fro,
And will not pause to count its own sweet gain.
I am so happy, that is all my thought!
To-morrow I will turn it round and round,
And seek to know its limits and its ground;
To-morrow I will task my heart to learn
The duties which shall spring from such a seed,
And where it must be sown, and how be wrought —
But oh! this reckless bliss is bliss indeed!
And for one day I choose to seal the urn
Wherein is shrined Love's missal and his creed.
Meantime I give my fancy all it craves;
Like him who found the West when first he caught
The light that glittered from the world he sought,
And furled his sails till Dawn should show the land;
While in glad dreams he saw the ambient waves
Go rippling brightly up a golden strand.

Hath there not been a softer breath at play
In the long woodland aisles than often sweeps
At this rough season through their solemn deeps —
A gentle Ariel sent by gentle May,

Who knew it was the morn
On which a hope was born,
To greet the flower ere it was fully blown,
And nurse it as some lily of her own?
And wherefore, save to grace a happy day,
Did the whole west at blushing sunset glow
With clouds that, floating up in bridal snow,
Passed with the festal eve, rose-crowned, away!
And now, if I may trust my straining sight,
The heavens appear with added stars to-night,
And deeper depths, and more celestial height
Than hath been reached except in dreams or death.
Hush, sweetest South! I love thy delicate breath;
But hush! methought I felt an angel's kiss!
Oh! all that lives is happy in my bliss.
That lonely fir, which always seems
As though it locked dark secrets in itself,
Hideth a gentle elf,
Whose wand shall send me soon a frolic troop
Of rainbow visions, and of moonlit dreams.
Can joy be weary, that my eyelids droop?
To-night I shall not seek my curtained nest,
But even here find rest.
Who whispered then? And what are they that peep
Betwixt the foliage in the tree-top there?
Come, Fairy Shadows! for the morn is near,

When to your sombre pine ye all must creep;
Come, ye wild pilots of the darkness, ere
My spirit sinks into the gulf of Sleep;
Ev'n now it circles round and round the deep —
Appear! Appear!

FLOWER-LIFE.

I THINK that next to your sweet eyes,
And pleasant books, and starry skies,
I love the world of flowers;
Less for their beauty of a day,
Than for the tender things they say,
And for a creed I've held alway,
That they are sentient powers.

It may be matter for a smile —
And I laugh secretly the while
I speak the fancy out —
But that they love, and that they woo,
And that they often marry too,
And do as noisier creatures do,
I've not the faintest doubt.

And so, I cannot deem it right
To take them from the glad sunlight,
As I have sometimes dared;
Though not without an anxious sigh

Lest this should break some gentle tie,
Some covenant of friendship, I
    Had better far have spared.

And when, in wild or thoughtless hours,
My hand hath crushed the tiniest flowers,
    I ne'er could shut from sight
The corpses of the tender things,
With other drear imaginings,
And little angel-flowers with wings
    Would haunt me through the night.

Oh! say you, friend, the creed is fraught
With sad, and ev'n with painful thought,
    Nor could you bear to know
That such capacities belong
To creatures helpless against wrong,
At once too weak to fly the strong
    Or front the feeblest foe?

So be it always, then, with you;
So be it — whether false or true —
    I press my faith on none;
If other fancies please you more,
The flowers shall blossom as before,
Dear as the Sybil-leaves of yore,
    But senseless, every one.

Yet, though I give you no reply,
It were not hard to justify
　　My creed to partial ears;
But, conscious of the cruel part,
My rhymes would flow with faltering art,
I could not plead against your heart,
　　Nor reason 'gainst your tears.

LOVE'S LOGIC.

And if I ask thee for a kiss,
  I ask no more than this sweet breeze,
With far less title to the bliss,
  Steals every minute at his ease.
And yet how placid is thy brow!
  It seems to woo the bold caress,
While now he takes his kiss, and now
  All sorts of freedoms with thy dress.

Or if I dare thy hand to touch,
  Hath nothing pressed its palm before?
A flower, I'm sure, hath done as much,
  And ah! some senseless diamond more.
It strikes me, Love, the very rings,
  Now sparkling on that hand of thine,
Could tell some truly startling things,
  If they had tongues or touch like mine.

Indeed, indeed, I do not know
  Of all that thou hast power to grant,

A boon for which I could not show
  Some pretty precedent extant.
Suppose, for instance, I should clasp
  Thus, — so, — and thus ! — thy slender waist —
I would not hold within my grasp
  More than this loosened zone embraced.

Oh ! put the anger from thine eyes,
  Or shut them if they still must frown ;
Those lids, despite yon garish skies,
  Can bring a timely darkness down.
Then, if in that convenient night,
  My lips should press thy dewy mouth,
The touch shall be so soft, so light,
  Thou'lt fancy me — this gentle South.

YOUTH AND MANHOOD.

ANOTHER year! — a short one, if it flow
Like that just past, —
And I shall stand — if years can make me so —
A man at last.

Yet, while the hours permit me, I would pause
And contemplate
The lot whereto unalterable laws
Have bound my fate.

Yet, from the starry regions of my youth,
The empyreal height,
Where dreams are happiness, and feeling truth,
And life delight —

From that ethereal and serene abode,
My soul would gaze
Downwards upon the wide and winding road,
Where manhood plays;

Plays with the baubles and the gauds of earth —
 Wealth, power, and fame —
Nor knows that in the twelvemonth after birth
 He did the same.

Where the descent begins, through long defiles
 I see them wind;
And some are looking down with hopeful smiles,
 And some are — blind.

And farther on a gay and glorious green
 Dazzles the sight,
While noble forms are moving o'er the scene,
 Like things of light.

Towers, temples, domes of perfect symmetry,
 Rise broad and high,
With pinnacles among the clouds; — ah me!
 None touch the sky.

None pierce the pure and lofty atmosphere
 Which I breathe now —
And the strong spirits that inhabit there,
 Live — God sees how.

Sick of the very treasure which they heap;
 Their tearless eyes

Sealed ever in a heaven-forgetting sleep
    Whose dreams are lies.

And so, a motley, unattractive throng,
    They toil and plod,
Dead to the holy ecstacies of song,
    To love and God.

Dear God! if that I may not keep through life
    My trust, my truth,
And that I must, in yonder endless strife,
    Lose faith with youth —

If the same toil which indurates the hand
    Must steel the heart,
Till, in the wonders of the Ideal Land,
    It have no part —

Oh! take me hence! I would no longer stay
    Beneath the sky;
Give me to chant one pure and deathless lay,
    And let me die!

TO WHOM?

AWAKE upon a couch of pain,
  I see a star betwixt the trees;
Across yon darkening field of cane,
  Comes slow and soft the evening breeze.
My curtain's folds are faintly stirred;
  And moving lightly in her rest,
I hear the chirrup of a bird,
  That dreameth in some neighboring nest.

Last night I took no note of these —
  How it was passed I scarce can say;
'Twas not in prayers to Heaven for ease,
  'Twas not in wishes for the day.
Impatient tears, and passionate sighs,
  Touched as with fire the pulse of pain, —
I cursed, and cursed the wildering eyes
  That burned this fever in my brain.

Oh! blessings on the quiet hour!
  My thoughts in calmer current flow;
She is not conscious of her power,
  And hath no knowledge of my woe.

Perhaps, if like yon peaceful star,
  She looked upon my burning brow,
She would not pity from afar,
  But kiss me as the breeze does now.

TO THEE.

DRAW close the lattice and the door!
  Shut out the very stars above!
No other eyes than mine shall pore
  Upon this thrilling tale of love.
As, since the book was open last,
  Along its dear and sacred text,
No other eyes than thine have passed —
  Be mine the eyes that trace it next!

Oh! very nobly is it wrought, —
  This web of love's divinest light, —
But not to feed my soul with thought,
  Hang I upon the book to-night;
I read it only for thy sake,
  To every page my lips I press —
The very leaves appear to make
  A silken rustle like thy dress.

And so, as each blest page I turn,
  I seem, with many a secret thrill,
To touch a soft white hand, and burn
  To clasp and kiss it at my will.

Oh! if a fancy be so sweet
  These shadowy fingers touching mine—
How wildly would my pulses beat,
  If they *could* feel the beat of thine!

HYMN.

SUNG AT THE CONSECRATION OF MAGNOLIA CEMETERY, CHARLESTON, (S. C.)

WHOSE was the hand that painted thee, O Death!
In the false aspect of a ruthless foe,
Despair and sorrow waiting on thy breath —
O gentle Power! who could have wronged thee so?

Thou rather should'st be crowned with fadeless flowers,
Of lasting fragrance and celestial hue;
Or be thy couch amid funereal bowers,
But let the stars and sunlight sparkle through.

So, with these thoughts before us, we have fixed
And beautified, O Death! thy mansion here,
Where gloom and gladness — grave and garden — mixed,
Make it a place to love, and not to fear.

Heaven! shed thy most propitious dews around!
  Ye holy stars! look down with tender eyes,
And gild and guard, and consecrate the ground
  Where we may rest, and whence we pray to rise.

STANZAS.

A MOTHER GAZES UPON HER DAUGHTER, ARRAYED FOR AN APPROACHING BRIDAL. WRITTEN IN ILLUSTRATION OF A TABLEAU VIVANT.

Is she not lovely! Oh! when, long ago,
My own dead mother gazed upon my face,
As I stood blushing near in bridal snow,
I had not half her beauty and her grace.

Yet that fond mother praised, the world caressed
And *one* adored me — how shall *he* who soon
Shall wear my gentle flower upon his breast,
Prize to its utmost worth the priceless boon?

Shall he not gird her, guard her, make her rich,
(Not as the world is rich, in outward show,)
With all the love and watchful kindness which
A wise and tender manhood may bestow.

Oh! I shall part from her with many tears,
My earthly treasure, pure and undefiled!
And not without a weight of anxious fears
For the new future of my darling child.

And yet — for well I know that virgin heart —
No wifely duty will she leave undone;
Nor will her love neglect that woman's art
Which courts and keeps a love already won.

In no light girlish levity she goes
Unto the altar where they wait her now,
But with a thoughtful, prayerful heart that knows
The solemn purport of a marriage vow.

And she will keep, with all her soul's deep truth,
The lightest pledge which binds her love and life;
And she will be — no less in age than youth —
My noble child will be — a noble wife.

And he, her lover! husband! what of him?
Yes, he will shield, I think, my bud from blight!
Yet griefs will come — enough! my eyes are dim
With tears I must not shed, at least, to-night.

Bless thee, my daughter! — Oh! she is so fair! —
Heaven bend above thee with its starriest skies!
And make thee truly all thou dost appear
Unto a lover's and thy mother's eyes!

FLORABEL.

O Florabel! I know you well!
  You cannot cheat me with your smiles;
That downcast lash, those sidelong looks,
  Are baits to catch me in your wiles.
And spite of all you would affect,
  And all that distant mien denies,
I read what you would never tell,
  In the arch beauty of your eyes.

O Florabel! I know you well!
  Your voice is very sweet and low;
But, right or wrong, I dare to think
  It is by no means always so.
And you can talk, as ladies talk,
  Of stars, and gems, and flowers, and books,
But I am very sure I see
  Less thought than mischief in your looks.

Yes, Florabel! I know you well!
  I read at sight each girlish art;
When that sweet brow is most sedate,
  I know you're laughing in your heart.

And when you turn to hear me speak,
  And seem so very pleased to hear,
I guess the jest upon myself
  You're keeping for another's ear.

O Florabel! I know you well!
  You love to flatter and to please,
But at your home I do suspect
  They call you plague, and scold, and tease,
With names I do not care to speak,
  Lest you should turn them into praise, —
In short, to sum my charges up,
  You have the most provoking ways.

O Florabel! 'twould please me well
  To see you once or twice alone;
Concealed behind a curtain, I
  Might catch at last a natural tone.
I hate the art that veils each thought,
  I am not cheated by your wiles;
You have not touched my heart at all,
  And shall not blind me with your smiles.

BABY'S AGE.

SHE came with April blooms and showers;
We count her little life by flowers.
As buds the rose upon her cheek,
We choose a flower for every week.
A week of hyacinths, we say,
And one of heart's-ease, ushered May;
And then because two wishes met
Upon the rose and violet —
I liked the Beauty, Kate the Nun —
The violet and the rose count one.
A week the apple marked with white;
A week the lily scored in light;
Red poppies closed May's happy moon,
And tulips this blue week in June.
Here end as yet the flowery links;
To-day begins the week of pinks;
But soon — so grave, and deep, and wise,
The meaning grows in Baby's eyes,
So *very* deep for Baby's age —
We think to date a week with sage!

THE STREAM IS FLOWING FROM THE WEST.

THE stream is flowing from the west;
  As if it poured from yonder skies,
It wears upon its rippling breast
  The sunset's golden dyes;
And bearing onward to the sea,
'Twill clasp the isle that holdeth thee.

I dip my hand within the wave;
  Ah! how impressionless and cold!
I touch it with my lip, and lave
  My forehead in the gold.
It is a trivial thought, but sweet,
Perhaps the wave will kiss thy feet.

Alas! I leave no trace behind—
  As little on the senseless stream
As on thy heart, or on thy mind;—
  Which was the simpler dream,
To win that warm wild love of thine,
Or make the water whisper mine?

Dear stream! some moons must wax and wane
  Ere I again shall cross thy tide,
And then perhaps a viewless chain
  Will drag me to her side,
To love with all my spirit's scope,
To wish, do everything but — hope.

SONG.

When I bade thee adieu, thou rememb'rest the
time,
To depart for no distant or alien clime,
Oh! who would have deemed, as I sighed it in
tears,
The farewell then spoken a farewell for years!

Yet, believe me, whatever those years may have
brought
Of deadness to feeling, or sadness to thought,
And whatever the shame they have stamped on
my brow,
No change ever touched my first passionate vow.

Still I've looked to thy love as men look to a star,
Which may never be reached, yet is worshipped
afar,
And always in gladness, and always in gloom,
The star of thy smile was the star of my doom.

I have bowed, it is true, before many a shrine;
Have praised, and have sung charms less winning
than thine,
But the song was ne'er more than a passionless
glee,
I kept the soul's language — my silence for thee.

And, indeed, if sometimes I gave more than a song,
Thou wast ever the cause, and must pardon the
wrong,
For wherever a blue eye bewitchingly shone,
I saw in its beauty a type of thine own.

That falsehood is dead, and these follies have
passed,
And again I come back to thee, dearest, at last,
With the feelings of one who hath circled the earth,
But to strengthen his love for the home of his
birth.

HARK TO THE SHOUTING WIND!

HARK to the shouting Wind!
  Hark to the flying Rain!
And I care not though I never see
  A bright blue sky again.

There are thoughts in my breast to-day
  That are not for human speech;
But I hear them in the driving storm,
  And the roar upon the beach.

And O, to be with that ship
  That I watch through the blinding brine!
O Wind! for thy sweep of land and sea!
  O Sea! for a voice like thine!

Shout on, thou pitiless Wind,
  To the frightened and flying Rain!
I care not though I never see
  A calm blue sky again.

VOX ET PRETEREA NIHIL.

I'VE been haunted all night, I've been haunted
all day
By the ghost of a song, by the shade of a lay,
That with meaningless words and profusion of rhyme,
To a dreamy and musical rhythm keeps time.
A simple, but still a most magical strain,
Its dim monotones have bewildered my brain
With a specious and cunning appearance of thought,
I seem to be catching but never have caught.

I know it embodies some very sweet things,
And can almost divine the low burden it sings;
But again, and again, and still ever again,
It has died on my ear at the touch of my pen.
And so it keeps courting and shunning my quest,
As a bird that has just been aroused from her nest,
Too fond to depart, and too frightened to stay,
Now circles about you, now flutters away.

Oh! give me fit words for that exquisite song,
And thou could'st not, proud beauty! be obdurate long,
It would come like the voice of a saint from above,
And win thee to kindness, and melt thee to love.
Not gilded with fancy, nor frigid with art,
But simple as feeling, and warm as the heart,
It would murmur my name with so charming a tone,
As would almost persuade thee to wish it thine own.

RETIREMENT.

My gentle friend! I hold no creed so false
As that which dares to teach that we are born
For battle only, and that in this life
The soul, if it would burn with starlike power,
Must needs forsooth be kindled by the sparks
Struck from the shock of clashing human hearts.
There is a wisdom that grows up in strife,
And one — I like it best — that sits at home
And learns its lessons of a thoughtful ease.
So come! a lonely house awaits thee! — there
Nor praise, nor blame shall reach us, save what love
Of knowledge for itself shall wake at times
In our own bosoms; come! and we will build
A wall of quiet thought, and gentle books,
Betwixt us and the hard and bitter world.
Sometimes — for we need not be anchorites —
A distant friend shall cheer us through the Post
Or some gazette — of course no partisan —
Shall bring us pleasant news of pleasant things,

Then twisted into graceful allumettes,
Each ancient joke shall blaze with genuine flame
To light our pipes and candles; but to wars,
Whether of words or weapons, we shall be
Deaf — so we twain shall pass away the time
Ev'n as a pair of happy lovers, who,
Alone, within some quiet garden-nook,
With a clear night of stars above their heads,
Just hear, betwixt their kisses and their talk,
The tumult of a tempest rolling through
A chain of neighboring mountains; they awhile
Pause to admire a flash that only shows
The smile upon their faces, but, full soon,
Turn with a quick, glad impulse, and perhaps
A conscious wile that brings them closer yet,
To dally with their own fond hearts, and play
With the sweet flowers that blossom at their feet.

THE MESSENGER ROSE.

If you have seen a richer glow,
Pray, tell me where your roses blow!
Look! coral-leafed! and — mark these spots!
Red staining red in crimson clots,
Like a sweet lip bitten through
In a pique. There, where that hue
Is spilt in drops, some fairy thing
Hath gashed the azure of its wing,
Or thence, perhaps, this very morn,
Plucked the splinters of a thorn.

Rose! I make thy bliss my care!
In my lady's dusky hair
Thou shalt burn, this coming night,
With ev'n a richer crimson light.
To requite me thou shalt tell
What *I* might not say as well,
How I love her; how, in brief,
On a certain crimson leaf

In my bosom, is a debt
Writ in deeper crimson yet.
If she wonder what it be, —
But she'll guess it, I foresee, —
Tell her that I date it, pray,
From the first sweet night in May.

TOO LONG, O SPIRIT OF STORM!

Too long, O Spirit of Storm,
  Thy lightning sleeps in its sheath!
I am sick to the soul of yon pallid sky,
  And the moveless sea beneath.

Come down in thy strength on the deep!
  Worse dangers there are in life,
When the waves are still, and the skies look
    fair,
  Than in their wildest strife.

A friend I knew, whose days
  Were as calm as this sky overhead;
But one blue morn that was fairest of all,
  The heart in his bosom fell dead.

And they thought him alive while he walked
  The streets that he walked in youth;—
Ah! little they guessed the seeming man
  Was a soulless corpse in sooth.

Come down in thy strength, O Storm!
  And lash the deep till it raves!
I am sick to the soul of that quiet sea,
  Which hides ten thousand graves.

THE LILY CONFIDANTE.

LILY! lady of the garden!
  Let me press my lip to thine!
Love *must* tell its story, Lily!
  Listen thou to mine.

Two I choose to know the secret —
  Thee, and yonder wordless flute;
Dragons watch me, tender Lily,
  And thou must be mute.

There's a maiden, and her name is....
  Hist! was that a rose-leaf fell?
See, the Rose is listening, Lily,
  And the Rose may tell.

Lily-browed and lily-hearted,
  She is very dear to me;
Lovely? yes, if being lovely,
  Is —— resembling thee.

Six to half a score of summers
  Make the sweetest of the "teens" —
Not too young to guess, dear Lily,
  What a lover means.

Laughing girl, and thoughtful woman,
  I am puzzled how to woo, —
Shall I praise, or pique her, Lily?
  Tell me what to do.

"Silly lover, if thy Lily
  Like her sister lilies be,
Thou must woo, if thou wouldst wear her,
  With a simple plea.

"Love's the lover's only magic,
  Truth the very subtlest art,
Love that feigns, and lips that flatter
  Win no modest heart.

"As the dewdrop in my bosom,
  Be thy guileless language, youth!
Falsehood buyeth falsehood only,
  Truth must purchase truth.

"As thou talkest at the fireside,
  With the little children by,

As thou prayest in the darkness,
  When thy God is nigh,

"With a speech as chaste and gentle,
  And such meanings as become
Ear of child, or ear of angel—
  Speak, or be thou dumb.

"Woo her thus, and she shall give thee
  Of her heart the sinless whole,
All the girl within her bosom,
  And her woman's soul."

TO A CAPTIVE OWL.

I SHOULD be dumb before thee, feathered sage!
  And gaze upon thy phiz with solemn awe,
But for a most audacious wish to guage
  The hoarded wisdom of thy learned craw.

Art thou, grave Bird! so wondrous wise indeed?
  Speak freely, without fear of jest or gibe —
What is thy moral and religious creed?
  And what the metaphysics of thy tribe?

A Poet, curious in birds and brutes,
  I do not question thee in idle play;
What is thy station? What are thy pursuits?
  Doubtless thou hast thy pleasures — what are *they*?

Or is't thy wont to muse and mouse at once,
  Entice thy prey with airs of meditation,
And with the unvarying habits of a dunce,
  To dine in solemn depths of contemplation?

There may be much — the world at least says so —
Behind that ponderous brow and thoughtful gaze;
Yet such a great philosopher should know,
It is by no means wise to think always.

And, Bird, despite thy meditative air,
I hold thy stock of wit but paltry pelf —
Thou show'st that same grave aspect everywhere,
And wouldst look thoughtful, stuffed, upon a shelf.

I grieve to be so plain, renownéd Bird, —
Thy fame's a flam, and thou an empty fowl;
And what is more, upon a Poet's word
I'd say as much, wert thou Minerva's owl.

So doff th' imposture of those heavy brows;
They do not serve to hide thy instincts base —
And if thou must be sometimes munching *mouse*,
Munch it, O Owl! with less profound a face.

ON PRESSING SOME FLOWERS.

So they are dead! Love! when they passed
  From thee to me, our fingers met;
O withered darlings of the May!
  I feel those fairy fingers yet.

And for the bliss ye brought me then
  Your faded forms are precious things, —
No flowers so fair, no buds so sweet
  Shall bloom through all my future springs.

And so, pale ones! with hands as soft
  As if I closed a baby's eyes,
I'll lay you in some favorite book,
  Made sacred by a Poet's sighs.

Your lips shall press the sweetest song,
  The sweetest, saddest song I know,
As ye had perished, in your pride,
  Of some lone Bard's melodious woe.

Oh, Love! hath love no holier shrine!
  Oh, heart! could love but lend the power,
I'd lay thy crimson pages bare,
  And every leaf should fold its flower.

HYMN.

SUNG AT AN ANNIVERSARY OF THE ASYLUM OF ORPHANS AT CHARLESTON.

We scarce, O God! could lisp thy name,
  When those who loved us passed away;
And left us but thy love to claim,
  With but an infant's strength to pray.

Thou gav'st that Refuge and that Shrine,
  At which we learn to know thy ways;
Father! the fatherless are thine!
  Thou wilt not spurn the orphan's praise.

Yet hear a single cry of pain!
  Lord! whilst we dream in quiet beds,
The summer sun and winter rain
  Beat still on many homeless heads.

And o'er this weary earth, we know,
  Young outcasts roam the waste and wave;
And little hands are clasped in woe
  Above some tender mother's grave.

Ye winds! keep every storm aloof,
  And kiss away the tears they weep!
Ye skies, that make their only roof,
  Look gently on their houseless sleep!

And thou, O Friend and Father! find
  A home to shield their helpless youth!
Dear hearts to love — sweet ties to bind —
  And guide and guard them in the truth!

A COMMON THOUGHT.

Somewhere on this earthly planet
In the dust of flowers to be,
In the dewdrop, in the sunshine,
Sleeps a solemn day for me.

At this wakeful hour of midnight
I behold it dawn in mist,
And I hear a sound of sobbing
Through the darkness, — hist! oh, hist!

In a dim and musky chamber,
I am breathing life away;
Some one draws a curtain softly,
And I watch the broadening day.

As it purples in the zenith,
As it brightens on the lawn,
There's a hush of death about me,
And a whisper, "He is gone!"

SONNETS.

SONNETS.

Poet! — if on a lasting fame be bent
Thy unperturbing hopes, thou wilt not roam
Too far from thine own happy heart and home; —
Cling to the lowly earth, and be content.
So shall thy name be dear to many a heart;
So shall the noblest truths by thee be taught,
The flower and fruit of wholesome human thought,
Bless the sweet labors of thy gentle art.
The brightest stars are nearest to the earth,
And we may track the mighty sun above,
Ev'n by the shadow of a slender flower;
Always, O Bard, humility is power;
And thou may'st draw from matters of the hearth
Truths wide as nations, and as deep as love.

SONNET.

MOST men know love but as a part of life;
They hide it in some corner of the breast,
Ev'n from themselves; and only when they rest
In the brief pauses of that daily strife,
Wherewith the world might else be not so rife,
They draw it forth (as one draws forth a toy
To soothe some ardent kiss-exacting boy)
And hold it up to sister, child, or wife.
Ah me! why may not love and life be one!
Why walk we thus alone, when by our side,
Love, like a visible God, might be our guide?
How would the marts grow noble! and the street,
Worn now like dungeon-floors by weary feet,
Seem then a golden court-way of the Sun!

SONNET.

THEY dub thee idler, smiling sneeringly;
And why? because, forsooth, so many moons,
Here dwelling voiceless by the voiceful sea,
Thou hast not set thy thoughts to paltry tunes .
In song or sonnet. *Them* these golden noons
Oppress not with their beauty; *they* could prate,
Ev'n though in cloud or star, of human fate,
They saw and strove to read the mystic runes.
How know they, these good gossips, what to thee
The ocean and its wanderers may have brought?
How know they, in their busy vacancy,
With what high aim thy spirit may be fraught?
Or that thou dost not bow thee silently
Before some great unutterable thought?

SONNET.

Are these wild thoughts, thus fettered in my rhymes,
Indeed, the product of my heart and brain?
How strange that on my ear the rhythmic strain
Falls like faint memories of far-off times!
When did I feel the sorrow, act the part
Which I have striv'n to shadow forth in song?
In what dead century swept that mingled throng
Of mighty pains and pleasures through my heart?
Not in the yesterdays of that still life
Which I have passed so free and far from strife,
But somewhere in this weary world I know,
In some strange land, beneath some orient clime,
I saw or shared a martyrdom sublime,
And felt a deeper grief than any later woe.

SONNET.

WHAT gossamer lures thee now? What hope, what
name
Is on thy lips? What dreams to fruit have grown?
Thou who hast turned *one* Poet-heart to stone,
Is thine yet burning with its seraph flame?
Let me give back a warning of thine own,
That, falling from thee many moons ago,
Sank on my soul like the prophetic moan
Of some young Sybil shadowing her own woe.
The words are thine, and will not do thee wrong,
I only bind their solemn charge to song.
Thy tread is on a quicksand,—oh! be wise!
Nor, in the passionate eagerness of youth,
Mistake thy bosom-serpent's glittering eyes
For the calm lights of Reason and of Truth.

SONNET.

WHICH are the clouds, and which the mountains? See,
They mix and melt together! Yon blue hill
Looks fleeting as the vapors which distil
Their dews upon its summit, while the free
And far off clouds, now solid, dark, and still,
An aspect wear of calm eternity.
Each seems the other, as our fancies will,
The cloud a mount, the mount a cloud, and we
Gaze doubtfully. So everywhere on earth
This foothold where we stand, with slipping feet,
The unsubstantial and substantial meet,
And we are fooled until made wise by Time.
Is not the obvious lesson something worth,
Lady? or have I wov'n an idle rhyme?

SONNET.

If I have graced no single song of mine
With thy sweet name, they all are full of thee;
Thou art my May, my Kate, my Madeline;
But * * * *! ah! that gentle name to me
Is something far too sacred for the throng
Of worldly listeners round me. Yet ev'n now
I weave a chaplet for thy sinless brow;—
Wilt thou not wear it? 'Tis a passionate song
Of a deep poet-life; and on it I
Have wreaked heart, mind, my love, my hopes of fame,
Yet after all it hath no nobler aim
Than thy dear praise. Ere many moons pass by,
When the last gem is set, the crown complete,
I'll lay a Poet's tribute at thy feet.

SONNET.

I THANK you, kind and best beloved friend,
With the same thanks one murmurs to a sister,
When, for some gentle favor, he hath kissed her,
Less for the gifts than for the love you send,
Less for the flowers, than what the flowers convey;
If I, indeed, divine their meaning truly,
And not unto myself ascribe, unduly,
Things which you neither meant nor wished to say.
Oh! tell me, is the hope then all misplaced?
And am I flattered by my own affection?
But in your beauteous gift, methought, I traced
Something above a short-lived predilection,
And which, for that I know no dearer name,
I designate as love, without love's flame.

SONNET.

SOME truths there be are better left unsaid;
Much is there that we may not speak unblamed;
On words, as wings, how many joys have fled!
The jealous fairies love not to be named.
There is an old-world tale of one whose bed
A genius graced, to all, save him, unknown,—
One day the secret passed his lips, and sped
As secrets speed,—thenceforth he slept alone.
Too much, oh! far too much is told in books;
Too broad a daylight wraps us all and each,—
Ah! it is well that, deeper than our looks,
Some secrets lie beyond conjecture's reach,—
Ah! it is well that in the soul are nooks
That will not open to the keys of speech.

SONNET.

WRITTEN ON A VERY SMALL SHEET OF NOTE-PAPER.

WERE I the Poet-Laureate of the Fairies,
Who, in a rose-leaf, finds too broad a page,
Or could I, like your beautiful canaries,
Sing with free heart and happy in a cage,
Perhaps I might, within this little space,
(As in some Eastern tale, by magic power,
A giant is imprisoned in a flower,)
Have told you something with a Poet's grace.
But I need wider limits, ampler scope,
A world of freedom for a world of passion,
And even then the glory of my hope
Would not be uttered in its stateliest fashion;
Yet, lady, when fit language shall have told it,
You'll find one little heart enough to hold it.

SONNET.

I SCARCELY grieve, O Nature! at the lot
That pent my youth within a city's bounds,
And shut me from thy sweetest sights and sounds;
Perhaps I had not learned, if some lone cot
Had been my birthplace, what the crowded mart
Taught me amid its bustle and its strife,
Of the stern actualities of life.
There, too, O Nature! in the home of Art,
Thy power was on me, and I owned thy thrall.
There is no unimpressive spot on earth!
The beauty of the stars is over all,
And Day and Darkness everywhere have birth;
The transient glory of a cloud may call
Thoughts of great deeds to us, and lasting worth.

SONNET.

FATE! seek me out some lake, far off and lone,
Shut in by wooded hills that steeply rise,
And beautiful with blue inverted skies, —
Where not a breeze but comes with softened tone,
And if the waves awake, they only moan
With a low, lulling music, like the rills
That make their home among those happy hills.
And let me find — there left by hands unknown —
A bark, with rifted sides and threadbare sail,
Just strong enough to bear me from the shore,
But not to reach its tree-girt harbor more.
O happy, happy rest! O world of wail!
How calmly I would tempt the peaceful deep,
And sink with smiling brow into the dreamless
Sleep.

SONNET.

GRIEF dies like joy; the tears upon my cheek
Will disappear like dew. Dear God! I know
Thy kindly Providence hath made it so,
And thank thee for the law. I am too weak
To make a friend of Sorrow, or to wear,
With that dark angel ever by my side,
(Though to thy heaven there be no better guide)
A front of manly calm. Yet, for I hear
How woe hath cleansed, how grief can deify,
So weak a thing it seems that grief should die,
And love and friendship with it, I could pray,
That if it might not gloom upon my brow,
Nor weigh upon my arm as it doth now,
No grief of mine should ever pass away.

SONNET.

At last belovéd Nature! I have met
Thee face to face upon thy breezy hills,
And boldly, where thy inmost bowers are set,
Gazed on thee naked in thy mountain rills.
When first I felt thy breath upon my brow,
Tears of strange ecstasy gushed out like rain,
And with a longing, passionate as vain,
I strove to clasp thee. But I know not how,
Always before me didst thou seem to glide;
And often from one sunny mountain-side,
Upon the next bright peak I saw thee kneel,
And heard thy voice upon the billowy blast;
But, climbing, only reached that shrine to feel
The shadow of a Presence which had passed.

☞ Any Books in this list will be sent free of postage, on receipt of price.

BOSTON, 135 WASHINGTON STREET,
NOVEMBER, 1859.

A LIST OF BOOKS

PUBLISHED BY

TICKNOR AND FIELDS.

Sir Walter Scott.

ILLUSTRATED HOUSEHOLD EDITION OF THE WAVERLEY NOVELS. In portable size, 16mo. form. Now Complete. Price 75 cents a volume.

The paper is of fine quality; the stereotype plates are not old ones repaired, the type having been cast expressly for this edition. The Novels are illustrated with capital steel plates engraved in the best manner, after drawings and paintings by the most eminent artists, among whom are Birket Foster, Darley, Billings, Landseer, Harvey, and Faed. This Edition contains all the latest notes and corrections of the author, a Glossary and Index; and some curious additions, especially in "Guy Mannering" and the "Bride of Lammermoor;" being the fullest edition of the Novels ever published. *The notes are at the foot of the page*,—a great convenience to the reader.

Any of the following Novels sold separate.

WAVERLEY, 2 vols.
GUY MANNERING, 2 vols.
THE ANTIQUARY, 2 vols.
ROB ROY, 2 vols.
OLD MORTALITY, 2 vols.
BLACK DWARF, LEGEND OF MONTROSE, } 2 vols.
HEART OF MID LOTHIAN, 2 vols.
BRIDE OF LAMMERMOOR, 2 vols.
IVANHOE, 2 vols.
THE MONASTERY, 2 vols.
THE ABBOT, 2 vols.
KENILWORTH, 2 vols.
THE PIRATE, 2 vols.
THE FORTUNES OF NIGEL, 2 vols.
PEVERIL OF THE PEAK, 2 vols.
QUENTIN DURWARD, 2 vols.
ST. RONAN'S WELL, 2 vols.
REDGAUNTLET, 2 vols.
THE BETROTHED, THE HIGHLAND WIDOW, } 2 vols.
THE TALISMAN, TWO DROVERS, MY AUNT MARGARET'S MIRROR, THE TAPESTRIED CHAMBER, THE LAIRD'S JOCK. } 2 vols.
WOODSTOCK, 2 vols.
THE FAIR MAID OF PERTH, 2 vols.
ANNE OF GEIERSTEIN, 2 vols.
COUNT ROBERT OF PARIS, 2 vols.
THE SURGEON'S DAUGHTER, CASTLE DANGEROUS, INDEX AND GLOSSARY. } 2 vols.

Thomas De Quincey.

Confessions of an English Opium-Eater, and Suspiria de Profundis. With Portrait. 75 cents.

Biographical Essays. 75 cents.

Miscellaneous Essays. 75 cents.

The Cæsars. 75 cents.

Literary Reminiscences. 2 vols. $1.50.

Narrative and Miscellaneous Papers. 2 vols. $1.50

Essays on the Poets, &c. 1 vol. 16mo. 75 cents.

Historical and Critical Essays. 2 vols. $1.50.

Autobiographic Sketches. 1 vol. 75 cents.

Essays on Philosophical Writers, &c. 2 vols. 16mo. $1.50.

Letters to a Young Man, and other Papers. 1 vol. 75 cents.

Theological Essays and other Papers. 2 vols. $1.50.

The Note Book. 1 vol. 75 cents.

Memorials and other Papers. 2 vols. 16mo. $1.50.

The Avenger and other Papers. 1 vol. 75 cents.

Logic of Political Economy, and other Papers. 1 vol. 75 cents.

Alfred Tennyson.

Poetical Works. With Portrait. 2 vols. Cloth. $2.00.

Pocket Edition of Poems Complete. 75 cents.

The Princess. Cloth. 50 cents.

In Memoriam. Cloth. 75 cents.

Maud, and other Poems. Cloth. 50 cents.

Idyls of the King. A new volume. Cloth. 75 cents.

Barry Cornwall.

English Songs and other Small Poems. $1.00.

Dramatic Poems. Just published. $1.00.

Essays and Tales in Prose. 2 vols. $1.50.

Henry W. Longfellow.

POETICAL WORKS. In two volumes. 16mo. Boards. $2.00.
POCKET EDITION OF POETICAL WORKS. In two volumes. $1.75.
POCKET EDITION OF PROSE WORKS COMPLETE. In two volumes. $1.75.
THE SONG OF HIAWATHA. $1.00.
EVANGELINE: A TALE OF ACADIE. 75 cents.
THE GOLDEN LEGEND. A POEM. $1.00.
HYPERION. A ROMANCE. $1.00.
OUTRE-MER. A PILGRIMAGE. $1.00.
KAVANAGH. A TALE. 75 cents.
THE COURTSHIP OF MILES STANDISH. 1 vol. 16mo. 75 cents.
Illustrated editions of EVANGELINE, POEMS, HYPERION, THE GOLDEN LEGEND, and MILES STANDISH.

Charles Reade.

PEG WOFFINGTON. A NOVEL. 75 cents.
CHRISTIE JOHNSTONE. A NOVEL. 75 cents.
CLOUDS AND SUNSHINE. A NOVEL. 75 cents.
'NEVER TOO LATE TO MEND.' 2 vols. $1.50.
WHITE LIES. A NOVEL. 1 vol. $1.25.
PROPRIA QUÆ MARIBUS and THE BOX TUNNEL. 25 cts.

William Howitt.

LAND, LABOR, AND GOLD. 2 vols. $2.00.
A BOY'S ADVENTURES IN AUSTRALIA. 75 cents.

James Russell Lowell.

COMPLETE POETICAL WORKS. In Blue and Gold. 2 vols. $1.50.
POETICAL WORKS. 2 vols. 16mo. Cloth. $1.50
SIR LAUNFAL. New Edition. 25 cents.
A FABLE FOR CRITICS. New Edition. 50 cents.
THE BIGLOW PAPERS. A New Edition. 63 cents.

Nathaniel Hawthorne.

TWICE-TOLD TALES. Two volumes. $1.50.
THE SCARLET LETTER. 75 cents.
THE HOUSE OF THE SEVEN GABLES. $1.00.
THE SNOW IMAGE, AND OTHER TALES. 75 cents.
THE BLITHEDALE ROMANCE. 75 cents.
MOSSES FROM AN OLD MANSE. 2 vols. $1.50.
TRUE STORIES FROM HISTORY AND BIOGRAPHY. With four fine Engravings. 75 cents.
A WONDER-BOOK FOR GIRLS AND BOYS. With seven fine Engravings. 75 cents.
TANGLEWOOD TALES. Another "Wonder-Book." With Engravings. 88 cents.

Oliver Wendell Holmes.

POEMS. With fine Portrait. Boards. $1.00. Cloth. $1.12.
ASTRÆA. Fancy paper. 25 cents.

Charles Kingsley.

TWO YEARS AGO. A New Novel. $1.25.
AMYAS LEIGH. A Novel $1.25.
GLAUCUS; OR, THE WONDERS OF THE SHORE. 50 cts.
POETICAL WORKS. 75 cents.
THE HEROES; OR, GREEK FAIRY TALES. 75 cents.
ANDROMEDA AND OTHER POEMS. 50 cents.
SIR WALTER RALEIGH AND HIS TIME, &c. $1.25.

Coventry Patmore.

THE ANGEL IN THE HOUSE. BETROTHAL.
" " " " ESPOUSALS. 75 cts. each.

Charles Sumner.

ORATIONS AND SPEECHES. 2 vols. $2.50.
RECENT SPEECHES AND ADDRESSES. $1.25.

John G. Whittier.

POCKET EDITION OF POETICAL WORKS. 2 vols. $1.50.
OLD PORTRAITS AND MODERN SKETCHES. 75 cents.
MARGARET SMITH'S JOURNAL. 75 cents.
SONGS OF LABOR, AND OTHER POEMS. Boards. 50 cts.
THE CHAPEL OF THE HERMITS. Cloth. 50 cents.
LITERARY RECREATIONS, &c. Cloth. $1.00.
THE PANORAMA, AND OTHER POEMS. Cloth. 50 cents.

Alexander Smith.

A LIFE DRAMA. 1 vol. 16mo. 50 cents.
CITY POEMS. With Portrait. 1 vol. 16mo. 63 cents.

Bayard Taylor.

POEMS OF HOME AND TRAVEL. Cloth. 75 cents.
POEMS OF THE ORIENT. Cloth. 75 cents.

Edwin P. Whipple.

ESSAYS AND REVIEWS. 2 vols. $2.00.
LECTURES ON LITERATURE AND LIFE. 63 cents.
WASHINGTON AND THE REVOLUTION. 20 cents.

George S. Hillard.

SIX MONTHS IN ITALY. 1 vol. 16mo. $1.50.
DANGERS AND DUTIES OF THE MERCANTILE PROFESSION. 25 cents.
SELECTIONS FROM THE WRITINGS OF WALTER SAVAGE LANDOR. 1 vol. 16mo. 75 cents.

Robert Browning.

POETICAL WORKS. 2 vols. $2.00.
MEN AND WOMEN. 1 vol. $1.00.

Henry Giles.

LECTURES, ESSAYS, &c. 2 vols. $1.50.
DISCOURSES ON LIFE. 75 cents.
ILLUSTRATIONS OF GENIUS. Cloth. $1.00.

William Motherwell.

COMPLETE POETICAL WORKS. In Blue and Gold. 1 vol. 75 cents.
MINSTRELSY, ANC. AND MOD. 2 vols. Boards. $1.50.

Capt. Mayne Reid.

THE PLANT HUNTERS. With Plates. 75 cents.
THE DESERT HOME: OR, THE ADVENTURES OF A LOST FAMILY IN THE WILDERNESS. With fine Plates. $1.00.
THE BOY HUNTERS. With fine Plates. 75 cents.
THE YOUNG VOYAGEURS: OR, THE BOY HUNTERS IN THE NORTH. With Plates. 75 cents.
THE FOREST EXILES. With fine Plates. 75 cents.
THE BUSH BOYS. With fine Plates. 75 cents.
THE YOUNG YAGERS. With fine Plates. 75 cents.
RAN AWAY TO SEA: AN AUTOBIOGRAPHY FOR BOYS. With fine Plates. 75 cents.
THE BOY TAR: A VOYAGE IN THE DARK. A New Book. (In Press.)

Goethe.

WILHELM MEISTER. Translated by *Carlyle.* 2 vols. $2.50.
FAUST. Translated by *Hayward.* 75 cents.
FAUST. Translated by *Charles T. Brooks.* $1.00.
CORRESPONDENCE WITH A CHILD. *Bettini.* (In Press.)

Rev. Charles Lowell.

PRACTICAL SERMONS. 1 vol. 12mo. $1.25.
OCCASIONAL SERMONS. With fine Portrait. $1.25.

Rev. F. W. Robertson.

SERMONS. First Series. $1.00.
" Second " $1.00.
" Third " $1.00.
" Fourth " $1.00. (In Press.)
LECTURES AND ADDRESSES ON LITERARY AND SOCIAL TOPICS. $1.00.

R. H. Stoddard.

POEMS. Cloth. 63 cents.
ADVENTURES IN FAIRY LAND. 75 cents.
SONGS OF SUMMER. 75 cents.

George Lunt.

LYRIC POEMS, &c. Cloth. 63 cents.
JULIA. A Poem. 50 cents.
THREE ERAS OF NEW ENGLAND. $1.00.

Philip James Bailey.

THE MYSTIC, AND OTHER POEMS. 50 cents.
THE ANGEL WORLD, &c. 50 cents.
THE AGE, A SATIRE. 75 cents.

Anna Mary Howitt.

AN ART STUDENT IN MUNICH. $1.25.
A SCHOOL OF LIFE. A Story. 75 cents.

Mary Russell Mitford.

OUR VILLAGE. Illustrated. 2 vols. 16mo. $2.50.
ATHERTON, AND OTHER STORIES. 1 vol. 16mo. $1.25.

Josiah Phillips Quincy.

LYTERIA: A DRAMATIC POEM. 50 cents.
CHARICLES: A DRAMATIC POEM. 50 cents.

Grace Greenwood.

GREENWOOD LEAVES. 1st & 2d Series. $1.25 each.
POETICAL WORKS. With fine Portrait. 75 cents.
HISTORY OF MY PETS. With six fine Engravings. Scarlet cloth. 50 cents.
RECOLLECTIONS OF MY CHILDHOOD. With six fine Engravings. Scarlet cloth. 50 cents.
HAPS AND MISHAPS OF A TOUR IN EUROPE. $1.25.
MERRIE ENGLAND. A new Juvenile. 75 cents.
A FOREST TRAGEDY, AND OTHER TALES. $1.00.
STORIES AND LEGENDS. A new Juvenile. 75 cents.

Mrs. Crosland.

LYDIA: A WOMAN'S BOOK. Cloth. 75 cents.
ENGLISH TALES AND SKETCHES. Cloth. $1.00.
MEMORABLE WOMEN. Illustrated. $1.00.

Mrs. Jameson.

CHARACTERISTICS OF WOMEN.	Blue and	Gold.	75 cents.
LOVES OF THE POETS.	"	"	75 cents.
DIARY OF AN ENNUYÉE	"	"	75 cents.
SKETCHES OF ART, &c.	"	"	75 cents.
STUDIES AND STORIES.	"	"	75 cents.
ITALIAN PAINTERS.	"	"	75 cents.

Mrs. Mowatt.

AUTOBIOGRAPHY OF AN ACTRESS. $1.25.
PLAYS. ARMAND AND FASHION. 50 cents.
MIMIC LIFE. 1 vol. $1.25.
THE TWIN ROSES. 1 vol. 75 cents.

Mrs. Howe.

PASSION FLOWERS. 75 cents.
WORDS FOR THE HOUR. 75 cents.
THE WORLD'S OWN. 50 cents.

Alice Cary.

POEMS. 1 vol. 16mo. $1.00.
CLOVERNOOK CHILDREN. With Plates. 75 cents.

Mrs. Eliza B. Lee.

MEMOIR OF THE BUCKMINSTERS. $1.25.
FLORENCE, THE PARISH ORPHAN. 50 cents.
PARTHENIA. 1 vol. 16mo. $1.00.

Samuel Smiles.

LIFE OF GEORGE STEPHENSON: ENGINEER. $1.00.

Blanchard Jerrold.

DOUGLAS JERROLD'S WIT. 75 cents.
LIFE AND LETTERS OF DOUGLAS JERROLD. $1.00.

Mrs. Judson.

ALDERBROOK. By *Fanny Forrester*. 2 vols. $1.75.
THE KATHAYAN SLAVE, AND OTHER PAPERS. 1 vol. 63 cents.
MY TWO SISTERS: A SKETCH FROM MEMORY. 50 cents.

Trelawny.

RECOLLECTIONS OF SHELLEY AND BYRON. 75 cents.

Charles Sprague.

POETICAL AND PROSE WRITINGS. With fine Portrait. Boards. 75 cents.

Mrs. Lawrence.

LIGHT ON THE DARK RIVER: OR MEMOIRS OF MRS. HAMLIN. 1 vol. 16mo. Cloth. $1.00.

G. A. Sala.

A Journey due North. $1.00.

Thomas W. Parsons.

Poems. $1.00.

John G. Saxe.

Poems. With Portrait. Boards. 63 cents. Cloth. 75 cents.
The Money King, and other Poems. 1 vol. 75 cents.

Charles T. Brooks.

German Lyrics. Translated. 1 vol. 16mo. Cloth. $1.00.

Samuel Bailey.

Essays on the Formation of Opinions and the Pursuit of Truth. 1 vol. 16mo. $1.00.

Tom Brown.

School Days at Rugby. By *An Old Boy.* 1 vol. 16mo. $1.00.

The Scouring of the White Horse, or the Long Vacation Holiday of a London Clerk. By *The Author of 'School Days at Rugby.'* 1 vol. 16mo. $1.00.

Leigh Hunt.

Poems. Blue and Gold. 2 vols. $1.50.

Gerald Massey.

Poetical Works. Blue and Gold. 75 cents.

C. W. Upham.

John C. Fremont's Life, Explorations, &c. With Illustrations. 75 cents.

W. M. Thackeray.

BALLADS. 1 vol. 16mo. 75 cents.

Charles Mackay.

POEMS. 1 vol. Cloth. $1.00.

Richard Monckton Milnes.

POEMS OF MANY YEARS. Boards. 75 cents.

George H. Boker.

PLAYS AND POEMS. 2 vols. $2.00.

Matthew Arnold.

POEMS. 75 cents.

W. Edmondstoune Aytoun.

BOTHWELL. 75 cents.

Mrs. Rosa V. Johnson.

POEMS. 1 vol. 16mo. $1.00.

Henry T. Tuckerman.

POEMS. Cloth. 75 cents.

William Mountford.

THORPE: A QUIET ENGLISH TOWN, AND HUMAN LIFE THEREIN. 16mo. $1.00.

James G. Percival.

POETICAL WORKS. 2 vols. Blue and Gold. $1.75.

John Bowring.

MATINS AND VESPERS. Blue and Gold. 75 cents.

Phœbe Cary.

POEMS AND PARODIES. 75 cents.

Paul H. Hayne.

POEMS. 1 vol. 16mo. 63 cents.

AVOLIO, A LEGEND OF THE ISLAND OF COS; AND OTHER POEMS. 1 vol. *Just ready.*

Mrs. A. C. Lowell.

SEED-GRAIN FOR THOUGHT AND DISCUSSION. 2 vols. $1.75.

EDUCATION OF GIRLS. 25 cents.

G. H. Lewes.

THE LIFE AND WORKS OF GOETHE. 2 vols. 16mo. $2.50.

Lieut. Arnold.

OAKFIELD. A Novel. $1.00.

Washington Allston.

MONALDI, A TALE. 1 vol. 16mo. 75 cents.

Professor E. T. Channing.

LECTURES ON ORATORY AND RHETORIC. 75 cents.

Dr. Walter Channing.

A PHYSICIAN'S VACATION. $1.50.

Mrs. Horace Mann.

A PHYSIOLOGICAL COOKERY BOOK. 63 cents.

Arthur P. Stanley.

LIFE AND CORRESPONDENCE OF DR. ARNOLD. 2 vols. $2.00.

Christopher Wordsworth.

WILLIAM WORDSWORTH'S BIOGRAPHY. 2 vols. $2.50.

Henry Taylor.

NOTES FROM LIFE. By the Author of "Philip Van Artevelde." 1 vol. 16mo. Cloth. 63 cents.

Hufeland.

ART OF PROLONGING LIFE. Edited by Erasmus Wilson, 1 vol. 16mo. 75 cents.

Henry Kingsley.

RECOLLECTIONS OF GEOFFRY HAMLYN. A Novel. $1.25.

Dr. John C. Warren.

THE PRESERVATION OF HEALTH, &c. 1 vol. 38 cents.

James Prior.

LIFE OF EDMUND BURKE. 2 vols. $2.00.

Joseph T. Buckingham.

PERSONAL MEMOIRS AND RECOLLECTIONS OF EDITORIAL LIFE. With Portrait. 2 vols. 16mo. $1.50.

Theophilus Parsons.

A MEMOIR OF CHIEF JUSTICE THEOPHILUS PARSONS, WITH NOTICES OF SOME OF HIS CONTEMPORARIES. By his Son. With Portrait. 1 vol. 12mo. $1.50.

Goldsmith.

The Vicar of Wakefield. Illustrated Edition. $3.00.

C. A. Bartol.

Church and Congregation. $1.00.

Horace Mann.

Thoughts for a Young Man. 25 cents.

Dr. William E. Coale.

Hints on Health. 3d Edition. 63 cents.

Lady Shelley.

Shelley Memorials. From Authentic Sources. 1 vol. Cloth. 75 cents.

Lord Dufferin.

A Yacht Voyage of 6,000 Miles. $1.00.

Fanny Kemble.

Poems. Enlarged Edition. $1.00.

Owen Meredith.

Poetical Works. Blue and Gold. 75 cents.

Arago.

Biographies of Distinguished Scientific Men. 16mo. 2 vols. $2.00.

William Smith.

Thorndale, or the Conflict of Opinions. $1.25.

R. H. Dana, Jr.

TO CUBA AND BACK, a Vacation Voyage, by the Author of "Two Years before the Mast." 75 cents.

John Neal.

TRUE WOMANHOOD. A Novel. 1 vol. $ 1.25.

SWORD AND GOWN. By the Author of "Guy Livingstone." 1 vol. 75 cents.

ALMOST A HEROINE. By the Author of "Charles Auchester," and "Counterparts." 1 vol. $1.00.

TWELVE YEARS OF A SOLDIER'S LIFE: A MEMOIR OF THE LATE MAJOR W. S. R. HODSON, B. A. Edited by his Brother, Rev. George H. Hodson. 1 vol. $1.00.

GOETHE'S CORRESPONDENCE WITH A CHILD. [Bettina.] 1 vol. *Just ready.*

RAB AND HIS FRIENDS. By John Brown, M. D. 15 cents.

THE LIFE AND TIMES OF SIR PHILIP SIDNEY. 1 vol. 16mo. $1.00.

ERNEST CARROLL, OR ARTIST LIFE IN ITALY. 1 vol. 16mo. 88 cents.

CHRISTMAS HOURS. By the Author of "The Homeward Path," &c. 1 vol. 16mo. 50 cents.

MEMORY AND HOPE. Cloth. $2.00.

THALATTA; A BOOK FOR THE SEASIDE. 75 cents.

REJECTED ADDRESSES. A new edition. Cloth. 75 cents.

WARRENIANA; A COMPANION TO REJECTED ADDRESSES. 63 cents.

ANGEL VOICES. 38 cents.

THE BOSTON BOOK. $1.25.

MEMOIR OF ROBERT WHEATON. 1 vol. $1.00.

LABOR AND LOVE: A TALE OF ENGLISH LIFE. 50 cts.

THE SOLITARY OF JUAN FERNANDEZ. By the Author of Picciola. 50 cents.

WALDEN: OR, LIFE IN THE WOODS. By Henry D. Thoreau. 1 vol. 16mo. $1.00.

VILLAGE LIFE IN EGYPT. By Bayle St. John, the Author of "Purple Tints of Paris." 2 vols. 16mo. $1.25.

WENSLEY: A STORY WITHOUT A MORAL. By Edmund Quincy. 75 cents.

PALISSY THE POTTER. By Henry Morley. 2 vols. 16mo. $1.50.

THE BARCLAYS OF BOSTON. By Mrs. H. G. Otis. 1 vol. 12mo. $1.25.

SIR ROGER DE COVERLEY. By Addison. From the "Spectator." 75 cents.

SERMONS OF CONSOLATION. By F. W. P. Greenwood. $1.00.

SPAIN, HER INSTITUTIONS, POLITICS, AND PUBLIC MEN. By S. T. Wallis. $1.00.

POEMS. By Henry Alford. $1.25.

In Blue and Gold.

LONGFELLOW'S POETICAL WORKS. 2 vols. $1.75.
do. PROSE WORKS. 2 vols. $1.75.
TENNYSON'S POETICAL WORKS. 1 vol. 75 cents.
WHITTIER'S POETICAL WORKS. 2 vols. $1.50.
LEIGH HUNT'S POETICAL WORKS. 2 vols. $1.50.
GERALD MASSEY'S POETICAL WORKS. 1 vol. 75 cents.
MRS. JAMESON'S CHARACTERISTICS OF WOMEN. 75 cts.
do. DIARY OF AN ENNUYÉE. 1 vol. 75 cts.
do. LOVES OF THE POETS. 1 vol. 75 cts.
do. SKETCHES OF ART, &c. 1 vol. 75 cts.
do. STUDIES AND STORIES. 1 vol. 75 cts.
do. ITALIAN PAINTERS. 1 vol. 75 cents.
OWEN MEREDITH'S POEMS. 1 vol. 75 cents.
BOWRING'S MATINS AND VESPERS. 1 vol. 75 cents.
LOWELL'S (J. RUSSELL) POETICAL WORKS. 2 vols. $1.50
PERCIVAL'S POETICAL WORKS. 2 vols. $1.75.
MOTHERWELL'S POEMS. 1 vol. 75 cents.

www.ingramcontent.com/pod-product-compliance
Lightning Source LLC
LaVergne TN
LVHW021409110826
845150LV00007B/1850

* 9 7 8 1 4 2 5 5 1 1 1 4 2 *